MEDITATIONS ON THE SONG OF SOLOMON

RUMI-NATIONS ON DESIRE

The Song of Songs

Edward A. Vinson

WORKBOOK PRESS LLC
187 E Warm Springs Rd,
Suite B285, Las Vegas, NV 89119, USA

Website: https://workbookpress.com/
Hotline: 1-888-818-4856
Email: admin@workbookpress.com

Ordering Information:
Quantity sales. Special discounts are available on quantity purchases by corporations, associations, and others.
For details, contact the publisher at the address above.

ISBN-13:   978-1-956876-16-1 (Paperback Version)
                  978-1-956876-17-8 (Digital Version)

REV. DATE: 09/11/2021

RUMInations On Desire

Meditations on the "Song of Songs"

by

Edward A. Vinson

© 2016

Contents

The Heavens declare the Glory of God....In them He has set a tabernacle, a tent for the sun, which is as a Bridegroom coming out of His chamber." - Psalms 19:1, 4, 5

"I will shake all nations and the Desire of nations will come and I will fill this house with Glory." – Haggai 2:7

"As in the days of Noah, so shall be the coming of the Son of Man." - Matthew 24:37

"For your Maker is your Husbandman... and your Redeemer the Holy One of Israel, the God of all the Earth.... And this, to Me, is as the Waters of Noah.... My Love shall be immovable." - from Isaiah 54

Acknowledgements

Over many years my soul has fed upon the Word of God, at depth, where 'deep is calling unto deep'. The Depth of God to depths in us. I have been well served and well fed by many translations and amplifications of The Bible. I give thanks for the People of The Book who have lived and died by and for the Words of Life God sends to us to spread Love's Good Influence as portions of the New Inheritance God gives us in Christ Jesus. His Words have surrounded me and overflowed onto the Table spread for us to 'take and eat', to 'taste and see', how Good God is. Always the same, even in the presence of our enemies. For God, in Christ, has "overcome the world" for us. And so we must be, found "in Him".

Once a Seer prophesied that he saw me surrounded by many books. The first prophetic word ever spoken over me was from my wife who said that I would "write for God". To do so as some are called, we must come into our "right mind" and be "seated with Christ in Heavenly places". We must pull up a chair at the Table of Communion where His Word is served and shared by those who immerse themselves in the Spring of Living Water to give us living translations of God's Living Word. It is out of that rich, diverse fare where East and West can meet in sweet accord and find that we can dwell together in Peace, that God commands a blessing. Making it possible that out of our inmost being, streams born of His Spirit that is Love can arise and flow onto the pages of our lives to "make the Vision plain". The Vision without which "people perish". It is thus that, by The Spirit, the Holy Spirit, the Breath of God, the Ruach ha Kodesh, that morning by morning a fire ignites within these bones. And I am sent to "Go! Speak Life!" In Streams such Life flows out of me, in Thanksgiving and in "Imitation of Christ". I, as a child, have sought to imitate and to please "our Father Who art in Heaven".

I have written this in memory of 'imprinting' upon Jesus as soon as I was "born again"; and also in memory of those who have gone before us as pioneers to "make plain the Way". That we in our generations may run with the vision of His face that shines on us, turning the Waters of His Word into the Wine of the Beloved that once so captured Rumi's heart. In such a marriage of our minds with His, "the mind of Christ", I drink and have been satisfied. To, "thirst no more" and yet daily thirst for More of Him and not forsake "the Spring of Living Water", the "Desire of nations". I have found Him in Meditations on the Song of Songs, in Ruminations on Desire. And in "Meditations on the Psalms"; and on Isaiah in "Streams": on the Lover of our souls.

Here pause with me and drink your fill. "Awaken love" for More of Him, "Jesus the same", forever More.

———

Cover photograph "Sunrise with Cross" used by permission.

———

Interior photographs by author

Notes on the Title

After many trips sojourning in Israel with its people, and after living out a modern Odyssey of sailing to Israel from the USA in 2010, the author spent a month is Jerusalem in 2015 for the Fall Feasts of the LORD. The High Holy Days of Israel - the Feast of Trumpets, the Day of Atonement and the Feast of Tabernacles when the LORD's Presence makes Himself known to be "with" and "in" the midst of His people. In "tents of fl esh". Treasure "in you". Where He is found to be the "True Light that enters every life", found in our "jars of clay", within the dust He Breathed into, with His Good Spirit. He seeks to be "as one", "with us", to fi ll us up to overfl ow. With Wine of the Beloved, poured. We are "in Him", the broken and the poured-out, too. As He is, we shall be for God a living, holy sacrifi ce: we from His brokenness come forth, as New Creations, born of God, not of the will of man at all. He comes to be our "Husbandman", and we "the bride" of His Desire, "of Christ". He is our Peace, such Wholer ess found to be "the Desire of nations". He draws us to be by His side and fi nd a Refuge from the Storms - from "tribulation in the world". He sings a Love Song over us, inviting us, to sing a Song of Songs to God.

It was during Succot or Tabernacles after I suff ered an att ack on my ability to breathe and experienced a signifi cant reminder of being 'sniff ed out', stalked by a Komodo Dragon, a beast from the sea, that I prayed and the next day found myself in an open sukkah or 'booth', having an iced coff ee and a cinnamon roll. Suddenly the greater reality of "Thy Kingdom come" invaded my 'lesser' reality and I witnessed "the Mystery" that is "Christ in you", leap out of me and, "mighty in batt le", sever the heads and tails of dragons that were surrounding me, drooling poison and waiting for me to die. I was delivered by The Deliverer. Not long thereafter I was in my room and under the Infl uence of the Spirit, inspired to say, repeating three times, "I will not see death any more." Once again I had passed from death to life, from standing in the 'gates of death' to standing under the shadow of the Almighty. His Love, "Stronger Than Death", further inspired me to continue "Meditations on the Song of Solomon".

That evening, a new friend, a Papuan island MD from New Guinea, rejoiced with me over the Goodness of God to the sons of men in delivering us from our ancient "bondage to the fear of death". He invited me to come and sail up one of the major rivers of Papua New Guinea to minister with him to tribal people of the interior and share the Love of God for His people, His "one new man", all Israel. Once again bringing into play the phrase, "from Jerusalem to the ends of the earth" (Acts 1:8)

It was during this Feast that ends with an explosion of great Joy at the giving of the Word in marriage to both the land and the people, and through Israel to the whole earth, that I found my footsteps ordered from Above and Synchronized by Leadership from deep within, on an inner path, the ancient Way of "Christ in you", as one anoi2ted to partake and take my place beneath the bell called "Liberty". There, in Liberty Bell Park, I was enabled to again perform marriage vows in a ceremony which I both performed as a minister, and participated in as one who says, "I will" and "I do".

Such Freedom found, must be proclaimed "throughout the land, to all inhabitants thereof" (Leviticus 25:10). Such Freedom from the Fear of Death, the Liberty of Love made plain, made manifest, is meant for us to live out here, before the LORD. But to what End? "Awaken love."

The Words of Spirit, resonate; they tremble in our inmost parts, the hidden place, where mantled in Shekinah's folds, we find "the Pearl" that Wisdom, in the Spirit, Is. Some hide it all the days they live. Some open up the doors to More. And some still say, "Come follow me, into the Door, across the Threshold, in Love's arms, into the Place that He, God, has prepared for us." It's in The Name Kaduri ("The Rabbi Who Found Messiah") knew. His Name is in me now, for Good, and cannot be denied as Truth. The Psalmist says, come, "kiss the Son", but not for silver or for gold, not for betrayal, but for Life. For Love made known, the Joy of Love, the Peace that comes when He is ours and we are His. And so it was, and so it is, as written of, that "God is Love".

There in Jerusalem, I found that I was walking in the Way, upon the Waters of the Word, bridging the gap, the distance of "divorce" between God's people, and the LORD of hosts. To be a sign in Israel. I had been called so many things, the "Witness/Ed", a 'Talking-horse' like Balaam's ass, an altar boy, a living stone, a "tribal chief", "Chief-Least" among the chosen ones, a foreigner, an alien, an infidel. But more or less, prophetically, one sent with Words to speak of Life and death upon my tongue: "Choose Life and live." I hoped to hear, "I will, I do", in marriage to the promised land. As sons are "married to the land". With daughters who "awaken love". And so it came to pass, I did; and as a "Christian Sufi" speak, as one now married to a 'The Jew', and to "Salvation... of the Jews". Amen.

I went to worship as I did, 'went up' to worship and I did, as "Akamuri" from the sea, from islands at the ends of earth, a 'Seahorse' clinging to "the Branch", found pregnant with the Word of God and Words of Life to "freely give". One of my "sons from afar and daughters from the ends of earth" (Isaiah 43:6) had given me the Maori name "Akamuri". It was a Gift bestowed upon me by our son-in-law from Manihiki, a Cook Island Maori, a Prince among his people and "a Prince of a man" who calls me "Dad". The name Akamuri means to go up listening, doing worship. To "hear and do" the Will of God.

While in Jerusalem I kept a journal called "Rumi-nations on Desire", the result of deep and abiding thoughts on Love. It spoke of Leila and Mejnun, two legendary lovers of the Middle East. It contained notes on Rumi and Tabriz's Shams, on David and Jonathan, on Jesus Christ and you and me, as ones among the many called and drawn by Passion, LOVE that's found in "God with us", unseen but real, as the Anointed, Promised One. He comes again to be "the arm" of GOD "revealed", for us to "Come Forth!", leaning on.

Such Meditations got too long; they had to be divided up into two volumes. The first, as yet unpublished, is titled "Stronger Than Death". This second volume of "RUMI-nations" or "chewing the cud', brings us up again to "taste and see", to ruminate on more or less the Meaning of Existence, Love. God's Banner over us is "LOVE". God spells it out: "Come follow after Me in Love, the Way. Respond with. "Yes! I will!" and "Yes! I do!", in marriage to the Lord "with us", the LORD of hosts: "Behold," He says, "I stand here at the door and knock."

"Many are called, but few are chosen," so He says; and, "for few have come wholeheartedly. And few there be who find the Way. All have been bound by fear of Death and fear of men who wield the rod, the Letter of the Law, not Love, not moved by Love, not by My Spirit, says the LORD, but by traditions handed down that make My Word seem null and void. But some are sent as I was sent, to set the captives free from FEAR: False Evidence Appearing Real. And to sing over you in song, and light on you with "tongues of fi re", immerse you in the Fire I light. Till Streams from in your belly rise."

I have been baptized in this Fire, and come up singing Songs of More.

The heart, a bowl, a bud, a rose,

was pierced to heal,

is carved to hold

the larger "New Heart" given us

to hold the larger Heart of God.

As Portions come to live in us

we must decrease, "I" must decrease

that Christ may grow

to be the Jewel, Diamond, Hope

that fills our view

with More of God and less of us.

With all it means, to Be Alive,

"Awaken love"

with something New we have not known.

We know not yet what we will be.

 We have not been this Way before.

But here we "Go"

sometimes 'where angels fear to tred'.

Come, enter in

where these words point. *

But why even reference Rumi at all? Because he was a mystical Sufi lover of Life and the Beloved through Whom he found Peace with God, the God Who "with us" is His Son, Isa, Yeshua, Jesus Christ, Emmanuel. This Kingdom's Mystery, hidden, IS, "The Mystery" that is found "in you". Some never even seek His Face. Some do. "In spite of things that make no sense".

In a world too often found at war, Rumi was born in Konya, Turkey in the 13th century, where Muslims, Christians and Jews, and other wandering/wondering souls from the East made contact. Rumi was a scholar and a philosopher who came to dance and 'fish among the stars' with Joy. To dance in song, with wild, controlled, abandon, spent; returning, turning, whirling 'round and 'round, to come: "Come unto Me," the Master said. To come out leaning on My

Arm, of The Beloved, The Unseen, "the Unknown God" that Paul once preached in Athens, Greece. He is the One Whose deep Desire is to be Known. He bids us, "Come, wholeheartedly; and seek Me as a lover does, with such abandon as I seek - with all your heart and mind and strength. To love the LORD and love your neighbor as yourself."

God is the Friend Who draws us to Himself with Love, to be His friend. Jesus "sticks closer" than a friend. He calls us His own family. God's Mercy has a human touch - that of the Son of Man, of God. What does He say? "As I was sent, so I send you." While some still call it "Blasphemy!"; the blind, too often, lead the blind... into a way that seeming to be Good, is not, and only leads to death and hell. Some have been found, 'digging their own graves', to 'Fall In!' As lemmings will and lemmings do: Destruction waits, outside the Ark that Jesus is: "The Door" that we must enter in. God "will not" always "strive with man", "as in the days of Noah", now.

I take such Liberty to think, that God "rewards" those seeking Him, those seeking More than what they've seen. "The righteous live by faith, not sight." Faith is the Substance, Love, that burns, and is a Fire within these bones.

Rumi met Shams, wandering in hope of finding fellowship that points to More of God. Their friendship did. It sparked a quest, and opened up the door to more, God's vineyard set upon a hill - the Wine of the Beloved poured, in answer to man's need for Christ. Such Mystery, Love, filled Rumi and poured out of him.... With walls of differences brought down and all hostility now gone, I think of Rumi's songs this way: as "RUMInations on Desire": "Out of your belly streams shall flow", and thus our Jesus spoke of God, The Spirit Who is Love that comes, to open up the souls of men, the Well of Souls, to know great Gain. To set us "free indeed" from fear, from sin and death, to give us Life. He is our Shield and very great Reward of "More". With new songs coming in the night, the 'dark night of the soul' births Light. Our sufferings can turn to Joy, "unspeakable", ecstatic, full. The fullness of the Gentiles comes, that all of Israel be saved. I find that Isa (the Muslim name for Jesus) mirrors the Face that shines on us. And yes, Mohammed weeps for Joy from the Perspective he has gained. "The hidden things, shall be revealed." The Glory of the LORD shall come, its Knowledge cover all the Earth.

"Now to Him Who is able to do More than all we ask or imagine, according to His Power (that same Power that raised Christ Jesus from the dead) that is at work in those who believe, to Him be Glory in the called of God (in you and me) and in the Christ, Jesus our Lord, in all, through all, fulfilling all to overflow with Love for God and for our neighbors as ourselves, throughout all generations, now, and in the ages yet to come. Amen." - an amplification of Ephesians 3:20-21 in the Good News of the New Testament.

"Come, magnify the LORD, with me. My arms, spread wide, invite you; come." Thus says the Mystery, whispering, "I sing you to me; be come in. From the Beginning, it was so; and is so, till the End of time.

I am 'caught up', am 'caught away'
in "Ruminations on Desire",
that of all nations called to be
as close as Your Breath
Breathed in dust
that makes of man "a living soul",
"as one" as You "with us" are One
and Your Name One
in all the forms
the I AM THAT I AM so takes
to change us to be one in Christ
and as a bride.
The Bridegroom comes.
I ruminate upon Desire;
deep and considered are my thoughts:
I meditate and 'chew the cud',
the ancient Song of Solomon.
I taste and see how Good You Are
to so redeem us from our sins
and choose us for Your very own.
The Water of Your Word is Wine,
of the Beloved, on my lips
is in my heart and on my tongue.
As it is found within the Psalms,
herein I "Kiss the Son" and Live.
Come, "arm yourself with purity".
Take Shelter in the arms of Christ.
As in Isaiah fifty-three,
Your Arm, O LORD has been "revealed".
Lord, we believe.
Please help us with our unbelief.
Amen.*

SOLOMON'S SEAT

-Song of Songs 3:9-11-

1.

One greater than wise Solomon

Is "with us" now, reminding us

Once, Solomon

In cedar, aromatic, sweet

Built Him a seat,

A litter that would carry kings,

Even the Weight of Glory, His.

Its poles, in silver, had been sheathed;

Its headrest, in pure gold, to shine.

Its seat was leather, whisper soft,

Stained royal purple, in and out.

Who wears the crown, is "with us" now

As He the Spirit has crowned King?

Who is His mother, "coming down"?

Whose blossoms worn upon His brow?

Who seats Him here within Thy walls

Of Heaven's "New Jerusalem"?

Who hovers over us and sings,

Rejoices over us in song?

The LORD is One and G D's Name One.

Greater than Solomon, One comes

And bids us, "Come" and, "Kiss the Son";

"Be seated with the risen Christ

As bride, with Bridegroom of the soul.

Who comes forth as the sun does, Dawns

To wash us in the early Light, "dawn's early light"?

What "Victory" is within our grasp

And, in His hands?

2.

Beneath God's "arm", beneath the

wings, Bathed in the rays with Words

of Life, In feathers, hidden, bedded down,

We heal at depths beyond the seen.

He is God's Love, revealed and sent

To "heal the land"

To which He marries us, as His.

Only His Love can heal mankind.

Jerusalem has crowned Him hers And, with Him, us.

With Him, we are the "bride of Christ".

3.

Our "mother", "coming down", does this,

Swings wide her everlasting doors,

Opens her arms

And takes us to her breasts for More,

Anoints us with the Oil of Joy

To dance within her streets again.

Love comes on clouds;

We fly with Hope, like doves to clefts

Within the Rock

To 'take our place', "seated with Christ".

We ride in, carried, laid to Rest

Beside Him and beside ourselves.

With Joy unspeakable and full....

God's Joy has now become

Our Strength,

Always has been, always will be.

4.

Jesus, God's Wisdom, has come down

By Word of mouth, Life on the tongue

To be our Wisdom, found to be

The rudder, steering ships of state

To gain the haven, Heaven, sought.

Salvation is not far away.

It still is found, "with us"/within

The "New Heart" given, by "I AM".

I WAR

-Zechariah 14:11-21-

I war, a "Talking-Horse", in place

And, 'paw the ground'

And toss my mane

And throw my head high,

Bowsprit deep into the stars

I lift mine eyes beyond the waves

Beyond the seas that roar, the hills,

The mountains 'round Jerusalem,

Unto my Help, The Source of all

I find on Earth

To be disturbing to I AM

Who looks for Love and Peace, but finds

Instead, blood shed

And cries of great oppression, loud.

I know He hears my cries and comes.

Of this I sing and testify.

I dance in place.

I carry Yours, the Weight of Glory, On my back,

The Burden, "easy",

Your Yoke, "light".

With You, I pull

That Justice, like a River, run.

I run 'in place' and paw the

ground With bells upon my feet

inscribed: "Let Freedom ring
Throughout the land
To all inhabitants thereof!".
With bells inscribed
With "Holy Is The LORD"
Ring out.
Give Voice to this: "I am the
LORD's And He is mine and I am
His", Your palms engraved with
"Israel" As those God marries "to
the land". I war by faith in He Who
comes And is the King of my Desire.
I war to strike your heart with "Peace!"
And to impress you to "Be still"
"And know I AM, the Lord, with you
To be Salvation at the door.
Behold I knock upon your hearts.
But who will take Me in to be
The Lover of your soul and, More,
The All-in-all of everything that is or was
Or is to come
When I return."

I come with Words
To strike your heart with Peace
And, More,
To open up your minds to Love,
Your hearts to Mystery yet "unknown"
To be the known Love of our God.

I war within your walls with song,

To come and make a new 'clean sweep'

Till shadows of the past are gone

And all things are made New "in Him",

To come and to "Awaken love"

And to be done, leaving a Seed, my song,

In you

To grow the Mystery of the Christ

In me....

And then to undertake, at last,

A final voyage

To gain again my Ithica of 'Home at last',

My "Home Sweet Home" within Your arms,

The "everlasting arms" of More,

The Haven I have sought in God.

Along the Way, this then, most precious

I would share

As Portions of the Treasure found,

A Table spread, a Marriage Feast

Of such sweet Oneness, At-One-Ment

That I now bear

As Fire within these bones of mine,

Within my belly

Breathed upon

Within the ribs that form a 'cage'

From which a "Trojan Horse" emerged

To carry me within thy gates

Intending to Release my Love

To enter into you who are

The very "apple" of God's eye

Where now, "the seeds" are "eaten up"

By cancer, hatred, as it spreads

Into "the lymph nodes" of "the world".

I war to bring you "Peace at last".

For "PEACE" was given me, to share.

For this, I died

And live again

To come to you

And speak of Love.

Unbound.

I OPEN UP

As night comes on

The buds I knew not of

unfold.

As prophesied,

To them, I open up, to More.

Each rose, a gift

To find You hidden in the scents

Within the petals

Spent

On love

We open up

To More of You

To be in us

the blossomed, Promise

Of "I AM...."

Within the Garden, in Delight,

I open up each rose, to find

You, in the petals, spent on Love.

I am Redeemed, "for God so Loved the world"

This Way, the only Debt remaining,

Is "As I have so Loved you, Go,

give Love. Awaken love and Scent

the world." Songs open up

"the Wealth of... Seas", In 'timely ways'

Of 'making love', be Known

"in you" Beyond horizons of 'the Seen'.

SILENT SOUNDS

Silent sounds

The Witness in the stars

Above:

"The Heavens tell

Speak forth the Glory that is Mine,"

Thus says the LORD

Of things beyond, above our heads

"Too wonderful" to comprehend.

They crown us, speechless, with True Love

With Blossoms of Your Kindness, spent,

Without speech, raining down on us

To shake the world

Without the sound of any Voice

But Yours

With us.

So, silent sounds

The Song of Songs

Immersing us

In Holy Fire

The Joy unspeakable and full,

In notes announcing

Love is here.

We are 'abandoned' in Your grasp,

Within the grip of More-to-come

From such tents of such starry eyes,

Pitched just beyond our reach for More.

Your Banner over us is Love,

Streamed and spelled-out

To come forth like the sun, at dawn,

Over Life's "Beach"

To gild the City of the King,

Comes as the Bridegroom, from behind

The curtain that has hid Your face.

Comes from the Bridegroom, from beyond

The Borders we may comprehend -

To take us in Your arms, as God's,

Belonging to the One Who Comes

Rejoicing over us in song.

With Healing in Your wings, You sing;

You sing us to You in the night,

Into our "right minds", found "in love",

To gather us unto Yourself.

Here, we may run, may leap like calves,

Released from slaughter stalls and graves.

"Shepherd the flock for slaughter, marked";

Beside You, racing, Time flies by

From the Beginning to the End.

May we, with You, take Victory Laps

And come forth "more than" conquerors

To "finish well"

And be as You are, here, with us

With Victory over Hell and Death.

Be present at this Table, Lord,

And, 'in the beds' that we have made.

Be everywhere, Adored, as here

And "with us", as You are, "revealed".

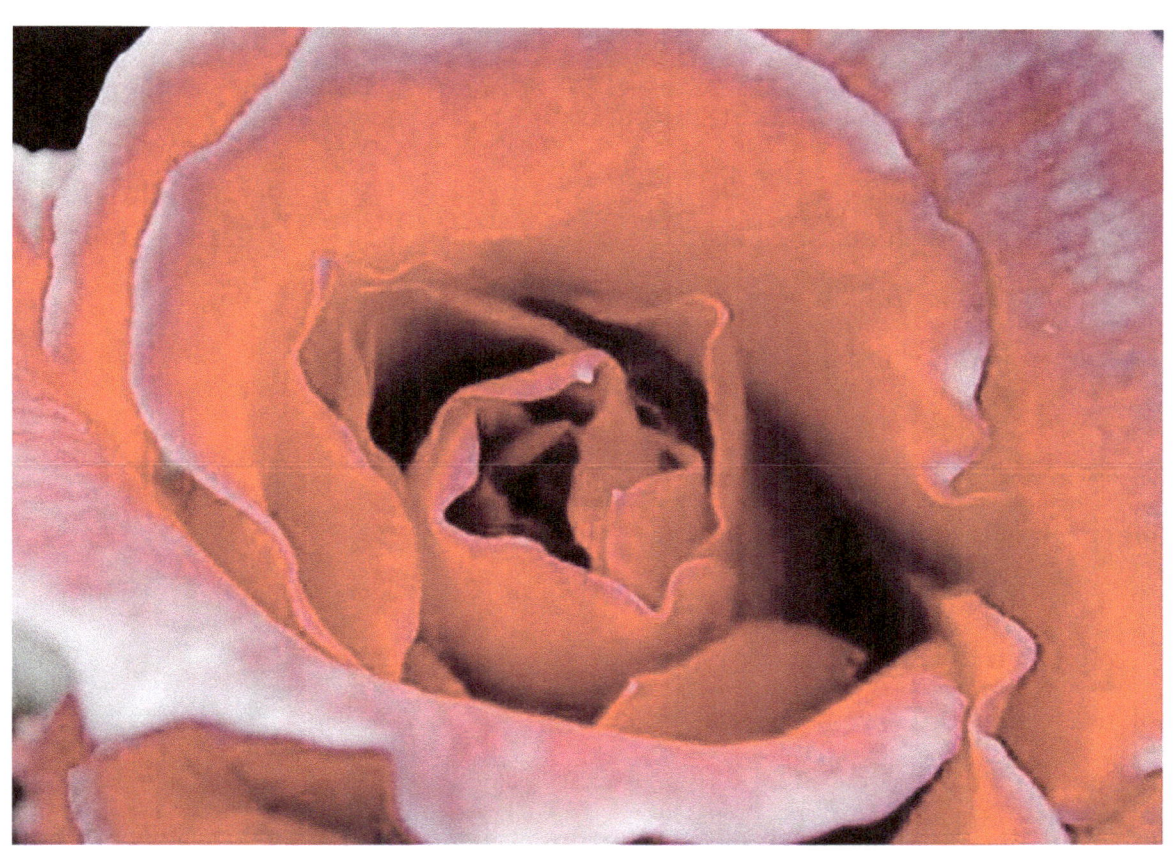

INTRODUCTION

By 'Way of Introduction', I

Would like to speak,

To whisper in your heart of Love

Of lives, re-membered, in God's arms.

I can't keep silent any more,

Can't hold my Peace, can't 'zip my lip',

Cannot contain the Joy I feel.

This old sea dog, is as a Bloodhound sniffing out,

The Trail God leaves as Man's Best Friend,

The "Life that's in the Blood" long shed.

The Scent I pick up, found "in you"

Is of the More-to-come "in Him"

From roses planted by "the Way".

The Way You Are, "with us", is Good.

Love wins and captures all my heart

And thus, "wholeheartedly", I come

Prepared to listen to His Voice;

It shook me to the very core

To "hear and do" the Words GOD sends

Through You Who are, His Word-With-us, Emmanuel.

And this is what He shook me with:

"Let there be MORE!" And then, there was.

"Cry out!" Love said.

This is my cry; these are my cries

That He has heard.

"I hear your cries and have come down,

To be "With you", by Way of More.

Let it so be: Let there be More.

Do not shrink back; do not now frustrate My Desire

To have and hold, from this day forward,

More of you, to find you "hidden" in My Love

Wherein My "arm" has been "revealed" -

"Who has believed" in Our report?

Who made you in Our image, both,

Both "male and female" as once formed,

Out of the dust, and Breathed upon

To plant and sow, be planted in the Earth, as Mine;

I AM "the Branch" revealed to be your Tree of Life,

To be your "Husbandman" of old.

I have proposed that you be Mine

For I was given to be yours."

Thus says the Mystery of the Christ,

Your Resurrection and New Life.

Some will refuse to 'hear of it' and, "hear and do"

Whatever Jesus asks of us, to make the world a better place.

But some will not refuse the Call; some will say, "Yes!"

And taste of Water turned to Wine.

Once, long ago, in "Paradise",

In islands in the midst of seas,

I stood within the "Gates of Death"

And entered in the Way of Life.

There I was carried, to receive

The Gift, from Him, of Peace, a Rose.

Its "Thirteen" petals marked the path

The Essence of our sure Return: "Life from the dead"

Through Christ, to GOD, in Heaven's Hands.

"The Thirteen-Petaled Rose" is His,

To off er, whom He will, the Gift,

The Essence of the Tree of Life.

As His ambassador, I come, with Invitation in my hand,

To off er you, The Healing in "the leaves", His hands.

He operates within the heart, looks on our hearts

As if we are to be His own, His "Chosen"

And His Bride-to-be.

His breast was pierced, as was the nightingale's,

For Love.

The petals of the Rose turned red

"For God so loved the world," this Way.

That are we carried, following; and, in His arms,

Found leaning, are, to cross the Threshold, inTo, "More".

Come with me now

To, herein, "kiss the son", our Light.

"Jesus, the Rose of Sharon", grows

One day and one note at a time

To be the Song within, unseen, and here and now,

To Live, "revealed", within the heart.

He leaves, 'Tidemarks', for us to share

The Answer to Man's Loneliness.

God hates Divorce from Who He Is.

This Invitation is for you

To be prepared to marry Him.

He is The Rose of ages past

That opens up, the 'Healing Process'

Of Love's Touch.

Bear with me, borne upon such wings

As bear souls over seas of loss.

Some lives are "Flight decks", thus laid down

To launch us, "storm-tossed", into Peace:

His Covenant, with us, is Love.

God's hands have cupped us, for Release.

So, who are these who fly like doves?

Some stand as "Watchmen on the Walls"

And in "the gap", between the Heavens and the Earth

Make intercessions in their songs, their cries,

That Love may be our portion here

That we may overflow with More.

Mixed with the whispers of Your Voice

With Waters of Your Word made Wine

Within this flesh of mine, I sing

And call down Healing from Above

To ease the heavy weight of Loss.

The Healing in Your leaves is ours

Is, 'in the Wind' that trembles me,

Stirring the waters that I sail.

The Process cups me in Your palms

Marked with the piercing of the Son.

You take us in, "Through Heaven's Eyes"

To be as Moses was, yet more,

And not alone, those "chosen" to belong to God.

Our lives are held to be "as one",

Each heart a cup, turned on Your wheel

Within the Potter's House, to be

A "new heart" formed, with others to be "aptly fit"

To hold Your Spirit, Love, as Lord.

We are to be, poured out on Earth

With More of You to share with all.

As it is, now, "in Heaven", found

To be the case in Kingdom come, "in" us, "in you".

Love's Process grips us, rends the heart

To shed the petals of Your Buds

That were, on Aaron's Rod, as "signs",

"In Israel", of "More-to-come".

Such petals, Lord, have strewn our path.

You know the Way we have not been;

You know the Way that we must take

To come to You, into a New Inheritance,

Through Jesus, into Life renewed

And without end.

"Eternal Life"

This is the Wine, of the Beloved, shared

And taken with the broken Bread.

And so I bid you, "Come, partake

To taste and see

The Love of God, made manifest

To be, "in you"

"The Hope of Glory"

Manifest.

We see, but "darkly"

As if through, a smoked up "glass"

And not through Your eyes, "Heaven's eyes",

The Truth

In Answer to the Question asked.

"Who is it, that you say I AM

Still burning, as I Am, with Zeal

Consumed to build My Father's House,

With you, My living stones, as walls?

Thus says the Lord, I gave Myself

To be as I was, lamb and ram, caught in "the bush"

And crowned with thorns,

Hung on a tree and mocked, as "King".

I now have come down once again.

Unseen, I knock upon your hearts

And would "be come in", found "in you",

Within your dust

The very Breath of God, with Life

That you become the "living" souls

That I designed to be My own.

For this you must be born again."

I have not been this Way before.

I see but darkly through a glass.

Our ways of seeing are not Yours.

Until the heart be circumcised

We cannot enter into More;

And once Your Word has been applied

As sharper than a two-edged sword,

Our "work" is simply to "believe"

And come, "as children" come, to You.

Your petals note the song I sing.

We sing together, here entwined.

Our voices mingle in such Love,

Beneath the Banner of Your Love.

"Lord, I believe;

But help me with my unbelief."

This seems to be "too good" to be

The Answer we have waited for.

And yet You Are and always were

The Answer to our, "Where was God?"

Of You, I sing

That it is You, "with us", this Way.

No other god has been with me

The Way You Are.

It's You! It's You that we desire

In all things, from the start, to be

The Sweet Beginning and The End

Of all things now concerning Man.

You are our "first love", last, revealed

In Purpose found, in following

Your Footprints on Life's narrow beach.

Has Man not been as grains of sand

Upon whom You have left Your mark?

Have we not known, and heard Your Call

To be a "fisher after men"

And pull them from the seas that roar?

You mark the Way; You scent the Way

With Life not Death,

With blossoms that have crowned us Yours

With "Loving-Kindness, shed abroad".

I took the Rose You offered me

And "Peace" was mine

To carry back

And, posit, here.

What do I mean?

It happened in a foreign land.

It happened on a distant shore

In islands in the midst of seas.

In what men long called "Paradise".

There, long ago and far away,

I lay me down to sleep and died

And yet I lived,

Was led to stand before Your Son

To hear Your Word:

"In spite of things that make no sense,

In spite of war and holocaust,

In spite of racial strife and greed,

In spite of pride, in spite of lust

And lack of love,

I have a Plan to bring to pass

And I will do it, says the Lord.

Here is a Portion of My Peace

For you to carry back with you."

And so, a New Way opened up.

Years later, I returned, to find

There, at the ends of Earth, a sign

Of blossoms in a pearl shell, carved.

And later, when my daughter died,

There, in the sand, an SOS

Sparked this, a question, from her son:

"What does is mean, granddad, to see

These letters written on the beach?"

"It means this, son: God, 'Save Our Souls'

Where we are lost here in such Grief."

The Pain propelled me, deeper still,

Beneath the surface of the seen

Until I now sing, full of Joy

A "New Song" that becomes a book,

That of my "Song of Songs", to You.

Tears lasted through the night, till Dawn

When Joy became my Strength, to live.

Where does it come from? Only You;

And others, where Your Spirit dwells,

In whom the Mystery, Christ, prevails.

Grief wasted me; in many ways.

Loss pierced my heart.

With Sorrows I, familiar, grew.

It drove me to a Vision Quest;

I come back with the Song I sing

To "make the vision plain"

And run; but not "away",

But, rather, here, into Your arms.

And if we are called 'mad', and found

To be, for the Unseen, 'lovesick'

For "the Beloved" and Your Wine

It is because the cup I drained

Became a Rose

And I am taken by its scent

To seek the Joy

That is "unspeakable" and "full"

Of Yours, the Presence, I require.

The Rose, a cup,

You offered, with Your hand, to me.

My simple, and one task, remains

To simply, as a child, believe

The evidence of You, "with" me.

You make my soul

A mirror of the cup You give,

White petals dipped in deep red Wine

Of The Beloved

That You Are.

They speak with Hope, of More to come

And fall on me with "tongues of fire",

Igniting me, immersing me in Who You Are,

Baptizes me, by You, in Fire

The Touch of which has made me drunk.

I never knew; I never tasted, never saw

Until I suffered for awhile;

Until, "established", I became

"Rooted and Grounded" in Your Love.

I never knew God is so real

And so 'up close and personal'.

Hard on the Wind, here pressed, I sail

Launched out into Love's unplumbed depths.

Rail down, my decks awash with You,

I am considered 'drunk' and 'wild'

And 'rollicking', an old sea dog

'Fresh off the boat' and, unfamiliar with the land.

As if I were at sea, in storm,

I stagger to and fro, in love.

And, lost in You, I cannot get my bearings here.

Until, as it so happens, YouWhisper to me, again, the Words,

"Let there be MORE!"

And then there is.

You offer me another cup

Till, 'full and by', I have been wasted once again.

I am "no more", as Enoch was,

As sober as I was before

I set out on Discovery's voyage.

Some have suggested, 'Sleep it off ',

But there, I only dream of More.

Oh, my Beloved, come again

And be made manifest in these,

The Rose amid the thorns of life.

Of You, we nightingales, must sing.

*****

Down through the ages, roses hold

The scent that has awakened Faith,

The "Substance", hoped for, yet unseen.

They are the source of ancient Hope

That gathers us beneath Your wings.

Roses spark us to 'waken love

And be, no longer, found alone.

Alone, we can do nothing, Lord,

That lasts throughout a long, cold night,

Throughout the "dark night of the soul".

Without You, nothing can be done

To ease the burdens that we bear.

You are the only Way that lasts.

Your face with many facets, shines,

A Diamond found within the dust,

Of Beauty that remains unmatched,

The "fairest of ten thousand", Lord.

Beyond our own capacities

Of Knowing Who God Is "with" us,

The Rose has come, to symbolize

The Union possible between

The LORD Who hates divorce, and Man.

The Garden of Your roses, is

Enclosed within

And found within Salvation's arms

With You, the Gardener of souls.

Those rooted in the Love of God

Conceive of You

In ways that are Immaculate,

On Earth as it, in Heaven, is

Not subject to vicissitudes.

You always are "the same" with us.

The Rose is both

Of this world and the World-to-come,

Both 'secular' and 'mystical'.

Such Unity is often, here, attained through loss,

Such Wholeness gained but by Your wounds

For "by Your stripes we have been healed".

The Rose evokes the Sense of Truth,

Where Justice, like a river, flows.

The Rose evokes the Scent of More

Where all souls find great Peace with God.

It comes through Jesus, with His Words

For who else has the Words of Life,

The True Light that has entered us,

Into our darkness, oft preferred?

What is it, that the soul desires?

And Who, by nations, is desired

Beneath the surface of our ways?

To whom has God's arm been revealed?

And who will, our report, believe?

I have been sent with Word of Peace;

The Rose evokes the Scent of it,

Though "it", be not an "it", but Him.

"Mystery" is at the center of

The words of one Farid... Attar"

A Sufi of the Story told, of Roses

As a Sign of God: Such "Mystery glows

With, "in the rose bed", "secret", "hidden

in the rose".

Of all things bright and beautiful

Love's Scent has captured me

With You.

I sing of Jesus, Sharon's Rose.

"The Rose of Sharon's Valley" is

A Planting of Love's Way "With" us

That always is and was a Song.

Do not uproot and throw Love out,

"The baby... with the water", tossed,

As trash, not Treasure,

Hidden, found, to be the Object of Desire.

Keep Him as He keeps us, with Love

For, "unto us a child is born

A son is given" to be King.

"Upon My mountain, He shall be

The Word that I have given you:

This is the very Word of God.

As it is written, so it is

And so He shall be once again."

The Scent of Love accompanies us.

Love would be, "with us", till the End.

It is so strong, that it will never be denied.

A "remnant" carries it, for God.

It grows within the DNA

Of those who have been "born again"

And are entwined, with Jesus, as the LORD's "true vine".

Roses have spread to all the world;

They once, almost exclusively,

Were in the Middle East

Found Good

As the 'most fragrant' of all plants.

They came to symbolize the Scent

Of Jesus' Passion on the Cross

And of His Resurrection Life.

Sufi s intuit much of this,

That every being, even stars, have nightingales

As You, the Rose, have us as Yours,

And we have You,

As Wine of the Beloved, poured

Into New Wineskins, us, in You.

How can it be?

All things are possible with God.

And Sufis have considered this

That the most noble nightingale

Whose "recitation" was complete,

Whose thoughts were most inclusive of

The well of all souls found on Earth,

Who sought to bring all beings in,

Through rapture to the Garden of

The Paradise of God's Delight,

Was through Mohammed, poetry.

As in the ancient "Song of Songs".

The SOS that Heaven hears.

The Union of

The Spirit and our flesh, in Love.

Made manifest, within the Injil, the "Al-Injil"

Of Jesus Christ, or "Isa", in the Muslim world

Of such "Submission" as is found,

Or may be found,

To breach the walls that we have raised

Against the Love of God

Revealed

In, "Love your neighbor as yourself"

To be the Truth

That sets men free.

I tamper with the 'course of things'

The 'heart of matters' found to be

The ways of men

As odds with all the LORD revealed.

I tamper with "Traditions" found

To nullify, make "null and void"

The Word of God sent down to heal

The heart of Man.

God's Prayer was this, that we "be one"

As He is One.

And thus the 'SOS' becomes

A "Save (us from) Our Selves", I pray.

For what good is it

If, in gaining all the world,

We lose our souls

In losing You

And are found Loveless in the End?

Moses, in anger, struck the Rock.

Then, "Jesus wept".

And now, "Mohammed" also, "weeps";

Is this "the Fast" that Heaven wants?

Has Heaven's LOVE been lost on Man?

What "Times" are we now living in?

Does Love grow cold?

How many fall away from You?

How shall our Fall

Now end in Peace

Except we find Peace

In Your arms?

Lord, once, You offered me, the Rose

And in its petals, I find "Peace".

The Rose has ever, always been

A symbol of the "More" we sense,

The "More" that we desire, of Love.

And then, in You, we find it All

And our Desire is satisfied.

Time out of mind, within the heart

The rose has symbolized the source

Of love's sweet mystery, a bud,

Unfolding, opening, to scent

The world we live in

With More Life

To take us into More, to come,

Return to You

As Joy unspeakable unfolds.

A taste of Glory, Yours, in us

Has come the way we are, to know,

At Your right hand

Such Pleasures found

In Knowing You

To be the Lover of our souls.

Some fear where we have been, to go;

The Scent we carry, smells like death

And bids them "Exit" where they are

And, for Your "Name's sake", "lose" their lives

To gain the "New Life"

Found

In You.

There is no other Way to Go.

"Do not shrink back to be destroyed."

Our "ways and thoughts" are limited,

In how, we may come

To "know"

You.

Lord, our Return is Your Desire;

We are "the Joy" before You "set",

The "Table", set

Where YOU were served upon the Cross,

Broken and Poured out, Bread and Wine,

That we may, "taste and see", True Love.

It never has been otherwise.

You are The Lamb, once slain for us,

Before the Earth's foundations, laid.

We look upon the One we pierced;

Broken and poured out, we commune.

Our 'little deaths', turn into "Peace".

And in the 'afterglow', we rest.

The Marriage Supper is complete.

In marriage, You provide us with

A bed of blossoms, full of scents

To symbolize

The Love of GOD

We find in Christ.

'Religious spirits' flee the scene

Too 'strait-laced' to be found entwined

Within the Branches of I AM,

Within the arms of Jesus, found,

To be so swept away, 'in Love',

And so Ecstatic as to be...

'Religiously' so 'Incorrect'.

Roses have come, are planted here,

Along the path.

They symbolize

The Way

We may be

'One with God':

'At-One-Ment' is quite possible

In the Atonement GOD provides

As Pictured

In

His Testimony

Found "in you"

To be "the Pearl"

Of such Great Value

That He died

And in three days

Arose again

To be "with" us.

The Same, for us

Is "in the Spirit": Be Immersed

And 'come up', found,

Desiring More.

"Let there be More!"

"And then there was!"

"Awaken love!"

The Time is ripe

For such Conception to arise

And spark a Love Feast far and wide.

Such things are Ordered from Above -

"Life from the dead" to all the world.

Let it be so.

Let Love be loosed,

'Immaculate Conception', found

To be the Order of the Day

With us, obeying, all Love asks.

God is a Spirit, LOVE, "in you" -

Repayment of Love's Debt, required...

"In Kind".

"Continue in My Kindness, come,

Return to Me, thus says the Lord

And I will surely come to you."

The Rose evokes the Scent of it.

The Mystery glows,

Where, in the Rose Bed, souls have come

To know the Lord, the Word, made flesh.

Some do not like it, not one bit.

So, "Be Prepared"

For there be "giants" where Love leads

To take "the land", of Promises.

And, for such Love,

The Lord himself, was crucified.

Be Hidden and 'Sub Rosa', found,

Under the Sign of Jesus' Love,

Unfolding, crowning us with 'More',

The 'Rosa Mystica' of God,

The Spirit, poured-out, "on all flesh".

And if we are

For Love

To be

Broken

And Poured-out

In His Name,

Called mad and found

To be, for the Unseen,

'Lovesick',

It is because

His Love is Real

More Real than anything

We've seen.

I have been taken by Love's Scent,

'Carried away', within Your arms,

Across Love's Threshold, into "More"

And am "no more" as I have been.

I issue this, an Invitation from Above:

Come, follow me; I follow Christ,

Into the "Song of Songs", propelled.

The Spirit blows us where it will

And with such 'Soul', we are renewed

To be Immersed, in Love, again.

RUMI-NATIONS OF DESIRE

-The Earth is filled; its Fullness is the Song of Songs-

"I will shake all nations and the Desire of nations will come, and I will fill this house with Glory.

The Presence you require Is Mine," thus says the One Who is to come.

"I came and I am with you now.

Let those with eyes to see, rejoice.

Let those with ears to hear, sing songs.

Speak with each other, to each other, with Love's Song.

Love's Silver and Love's gold are Mine,

to give away and make you rich

with Love's 'New Wine',

the Mind and Spirit of the Christ.

I Am the True Vine crushed for you;

the Fruit of My vine, crushed, yields Wine;

tears turn to Joy unspeakable.

Streams from My inmost Being flow, arise in you,

to overflow with Living Word, poured in and out of you, for Good.

Come, taste and see that I Am Good.

Such as I have, such Kindness give I, unto you;

continue in it: I AM yours, and you are Mine.

You are not yours, to do as you please, any more.

You must live My dreams, sent to you

to save your soul, from going down, into the pit.

Thus says the Master of the Field.

I plant you where you are to live, "ripe unto harvest", gathered

In My Name and arms, to be, to all the Earth, a gift.

I plant you to bear fruit that lasts.

The Earth, with you in it, is Mine.

Arise, and come turn on My arm; come dance with Me,

and save 'the last dance' for My Joy, My pleasure, says the Lord of hosts.

Save you for Me, "the joy" found whirling, turning into More that is

abandoned to the Love I AM

and have to give away to you.

We wrestle, you and I, as one; to come out spent, in one accord.

Given for you, give you to Me; and come forth leaning on My arm.

As Mine, you have a new name now

like "Jumping Mouse" of "Seven Arrows" sent to fly,

mount up as "Eagle", winged, to know:

come see me as I Am with you, the lifting, unseen Breath of Wind,

the Unseen now inspiring you,

to come up higher and to gain

such Vision on your Quest revealed

to be the "More" that you have sought.

"Let there be More," has come to this:

to Me, with you, and you with Me

where I AM found "in you", to be

the All-in-all of everything that you desire

that, by My Spirit, comes about.

It pleases Me to carry you, where you have been,

by ways you have not been before

into the Fullness of My Plan.

You dare not trust the sweetest frame;

Mine is the house I build you in,

no other 'framing' but by Faith,

The Kind that operates through Love.

None other but My Love for you.

I Am the Lover of your soul;

My mercy has a human touch,

to draw, by cords of kindness, Mine, with you.

Looking for lovers, I find you; so, lift the veil.

As it is written, "kiss the son".

Come enter in, to look upon

the One, the very Heart, you pierced;

enter where angels fear to tread;

enter My Presence through the Rent, the curtain of My body, torn.

The Door is open in My side; find Shelter in the Ark I AM,

the Tree of Life, cut down for you.

As in the days of Noah, come; I, risen, AM Salvation's Ark

Come into Peace; rest easy on My "arm... revealed",

the Captain of the Ark I AM.

Dine at the Captain's Table, come.

In Joy be found; turn, dancing, leaning on My Son

rejoicing over you in song.

He, the Desire of nations, comes.

He is the MORE of Love's Desire; and We Are One.

Be come into, the "New Inheritance" in Christ;

it is not in another, found.

And so you must be found "in Him", born from above; yes, "born again", from Heaven coming down to Earth.

Your "Mother" coming down is Mine, the "New Jerusalem" of God, the City" sought by Abraham.

Continue in My Way; be Free; be 'coming up', as I come down.

The 'sound of one hand clapping', is

a sound of your hand writing this.

What's in your hand, a board of Keys

To open up the "More" of Love?

What's in your hand?

A pen, a "ready writer's", Mine, a "Watermark"?

My 'Hallmark' is the very best.

My Best remains My gift to you, a Call to 'take up arms' and write.

A pen may smite a sword with Peace.

A pen may scent the soul with Love.

Go, do so, in My Name, with Joy.

And so, "Continue on" in prayer;

publish or perish, hear and do.

Shema, Israel.

This is My Word;

thus says the Lord your God I AM.

I seek submission, sweeter than honey, on your lips and in your heart, with My Word living, deep "in you" and My Words spoken, on your tongue.

And thus do you become My joy,

a blessing, sealed and sent, received.

Receiving you, I Am received.

Breath-born, now "Go" and "Speak Life" in My Name, in Love."

*****

By Grace, through Faith

Such 'streams of consciousness' are born

Within the Streams within the heart

That, by the Spirit, will arise.

With Mindfulness, be mindful of

The sound of many waters comes

To sweep us off our feet, undone.

The Wind of such Love comes unseen

To roar like seas

With "tongues of fire"

To light on us

In shells found empty

On the beach.

In such I find the roar of You.

The Lion of Judah on the throne.

The King, with More,

Is coming to have more of us.

"Let there be More."

The Word in all God's Fullness

Comes.

In waves that sweep the shore we walk

We, like the sand, hold Images,

The "Footprints" of I AM, with you.

RUMI-Nations on the Song of Solomon;

Mejnun had Leila, I have You.

1.

I sing You to me; meet me, Love

And smother me with kisses sweet

Until I die and live again

Within Your arms

Within the sweet Embrace of Love

I find I am too much alone.

Encircle me within Your walls;

Your Love will my Salvation be

The Object of my heart's Desire.

Desire of nations, come to me.

I sing You to me; come again.

O'ershadow me within Your wings;

Enfold me in the Mystery, Love

Of Who You Are - too wonderful to comprehend.

Come, have Your Way;

Submission to Your Love is sweet.

The whisper in my ears is You.

Your Love has slain me; raise me up.

Proceed with Mouth-to-mouth and Breathe.

Can these bones live? Yes, in Your arms

Ignite a Fire within these parts;

Breathe Your Life into these, again.

Without You, we will die of thirst,

Of hunger for the MORE You Are.

Without Your Kindness, none can live.

"Continue in My Kindness, come."

I sing You to me; meet me here

And smother me with kisses sweet.

Your Breath is full of my Desire.

Thus am I launched, sealed in and out;

My soul is on my spirit's quest,

Her own long, deep migration home.

Her Odyssey leads "through the sea"

Again, to You.

To enter in "thy gates" once more

And meet our Mother "coming down",

Jerusalem, born from above,

That city sought by Abraham,

The city built by God, not man.

Her Spirit frees me yet to soar

To mount up on such eagle's wings

To go forth and to win my wife,

To woo her and "awaken love" -

The loss of love restored to "More".

"Let there be More!" and so I say, "I do",

To You.

Yours is the "first love" ever known.

To You my soul flies, on Your arm.

2.

My way is through the sea again,

Is with the whales' and dolphins' song.

My way is in the air, to soar,

Mount up on eagles' wings, and cry,

The scream that is the mating call

Of meeting in the air, entwined.

Our hands are found joined, knitted, one.

My way is only found in You.

Yours is "in" me, the "Mystery", Christ,

Is in the mourning of the doves

Who fly like clouds

Seeking a cleft within the Rock,

The door within Your side, my God.

I'm coming home

To enter in behind the veil

Where pleasures are forever

More.

3.

Your city, here, Jerusalem,

In bondage to the "fear of death"

And "fear of men"

Is facing her "last enemy",

Is in her labor, groaning, worn out,

Bringing forth, through her travail

The Mountain that shall fill the Earth,

Cover, as the sea, the land

"as in the days of Noah"

Comes.

You hear her cries and have come down

Unseen

Within the midst of us.

Your unseen Kingdom comes with Love

Igniting fires within these bones.

Their "tongues" are licking at my feet,

Washing my feet.

Your Touch is bathing me with More.

The Fire of Your Love cleanses me.

Your Spirit washes over me.

My heart lies open at Your feet.

I pray You take it; make me Yours.

"I have been always and will be.

I was and Am and will be yours.

I chose you to be Mine by Word,

Am not a man that I should lie;

Am with you always

Yet unseen.

Unseen, in you, My Kingdom comes,

To fi ll the world you know

As Mine...

In all, through all, fulfilling all,

World without end

Within My arms.

In dying, merging, you shall live.

For My Name's sake, come, lose your life

And find it in My Love made plain.

My arm has been revealed to you.

Abide in Me and I will come abide in you.

My Promise is the same and stands."

4.

I bid you come.

I have a Song of Songs to sing.

A few short pages, then I'm done,

Burned dark, but lovely in Your eyes

Each as a daughter, as a son,

In 'likeness' of the One Who comes -

The One You bid us come and kiss

Re-membered and Remembering

With bread to break and wine to drink

In sweet Communion in the Name

Lest we, in our ways, be destroyed.

5.

The Spirit, in Him, is in me

The Object of my deep Desire.

I must have More.

I thirst for More.

I hunger that You be with us.

I am Lovesick

That Your Good Spirit

Take us, make us, Yours, indeed,

In deed here pregnant with Your Word.

I have been burned dark by the Sun

Found dancing, through the fire, by You.

I come out leaning on Your arm.

6.

My mother's sons, displeased with me,

Sent me to tend the vineyard here,

To water seeds and plants and vine.

But now the water turns to Wine

And I am drunk, undone by Love

And 'hopeless' now, for anything

But seeking You.

Tell me, Oh Lover of my soul,

Beloved of the Wine I drink,

You Who were crushed to give us drink,

Where may I find Your place of rest

And shelter underneath Your wing?

"Instant 'in season'; instant, out

My spoken Word has come to you,

Has come for you, to make you Mine.

If you have not had ears to hear

Then ask and I will send you Word

Of how you must be healed by Love

To love.

If you, by now, do not know

Where

I wait for you, an open Door,

Go ask the birds and animals.

They do.

They know "as in" My Noah's day

Wherein is found

The Door I AM

To enter into yet More Life

"Abundant", "full"

Of Peace and Love

Which is My Covenant with Mine.

Follow the tracks of those, My sheep

Who follow Me

Clothed in the white wool of My lambs

Who, for My Name's sake, lose the lives they have known?

To gain New Life, follow their tracks.

Like "Footprints in the Sand" I AM

The Unseen, with you, "Through It All".

Sing like the Wind sings through the leaves

"For healing" of "the lost", not found.

Run with the Breath that makes you Mine

In the direction I Am found.

The Wind blows where it pleases God.

Go where your 'pleasure' pleases Him,

Where streams arise that make Him Glad.

In the direction of the Wind.

In that Direction, I send you.

As I was sent, so I send you.

Where am I now?

Come seek Me while I may be found...

Here in your heart and on your tongue.

Go and "speak Life".

Mount up and ride; like horses, run.

Like riders of My whales, wade in;

Beneath the surface, disappear

To rise, found dripping wet with Love.

My dove descends to light on you.

A rainbow robes you

Rocking gently in the mouth

Of streams that rise

From in My Being, says the LORD.

Thus are you marked

For Life, for Love, for Liberty.

In Joy that is unspeakable

Full of the Glory of I AM.

I give you Voice, sent with My Word,

"The King's Speech" in your mouth is Mine.

Why do you shrink back, stuttering?

Why do you falter, fall back, shy away, retreat

From where I carry you in Love,

Across the Threshold into More?

Do not shrink back; be still and know.

Stand still and see

Salvation in the Love of God, the Love I Am

And give to you, to give away.

Go and do likewise, healing lives.

You gave me your heart; Mine is yours

To go, be as I AM, with you -

With others as a sign of More.

I lift your face within My hands.

The kisses of My mouth are sweet.

Your neck, bejeweled with rings and chains,

Shines like the Star I AM for you.

I draw you closer than you've been

To know Me More than you have known.

Do not shrink back to fall away."

7.

Scented You are

Upon

And deep

Within my heart.

My breast is scented with Your scent

And blossoms cluster in its pools.

How beautiful You are to me,

The Unseen, All-in-all of God.

You are to me now everything.

How beautiful Your feet remain

Upon the land I'm married to.

Your eyes, like doves, sing over us,

Rejoicing in Communion shared -

O'ershadow me and I am hidden in Your hand,

Our names "engraved" upon Your palms.

Cupped I am held to be poured out

To flood You with my praise of More

Yes, More of You

Is my Desire.

At Your right hand

Ten thousand pleasures flood my soul

And I am swept away in tears.

Your Joy undoes me as I am;

Stripped naked I am clothed with More.

I am a lily, glowing, white

Sway like a reed within a Breath

Of Wind

That You have Breathed in me, Oh King.

I am o'ershadowed by Your wings;

Your branches, arms,

With "leaves for healing",

Hands laid on

Have healed my deepest wounds of loss.

For Your lost Love, I was so Lovesick

That I died.

8.

I searched, but could not find You Lord.

I thirsted for Your Waterbrooks,

Became a valley of dry bones

And there You opened up my graves

And I arose, re-membered, one

To, as a child, remember You; and as a man

Remember and re-member Yours.

Stronger than death, my spirit, clothed in Love, delights;

Your shadow is my sweet delight.

In You I do delight my soul.

Your arm anoints my head with Oil

Until my cup is overflowed, is flooded

With the Wine of MORE.

Your hand and arm awaken love.

Upon the heights, my head is cradled on Your breast.

Your Spirit lives within this tent,

As Treasure in a jar of clay.

Broken and poured out, I am Yours

And You, "the same", are now found mine.

I tremble in my inmost parts,

Am taken in the Awe of God.

9.

I charge you, daughters,

'Waken love.

Awaken love.

Arise and cry out, here, He comes;

His Kingdom comes, unseen, in me

'Till I am pregnant with the Word

Breasting the mountains, leaping the hills

And seeking after you, He speaks.

"Speak Life," He says,

"Arise and come away with Me.

Winter is past; the rains are gone.

The desert blooms, your heart renews

The ancient vows

Of marriage to the land and God.

The singing of the birds is here.

The doves are moaning, sick for love.

Lovesick I Am

For More of you.

Daughters of Zion, 'waken love

To know the "More"

Of Your desire - your Maker

And your Husbandman,

Thus says the Lord."

Thus whispers God.

My heart is full of More-to-come.

The figs grow ripe

With seed with which to seed the Earth,

Even its dust, to taste and see.

The dew upon Your lips is sweet.

The Vine drips fragrance, fills the air

Entwining now, heavy with fruit

Like breasts You are

The "Many-Breasted One" of dreams

That keep the soul

Of many

From the pit that waits.

You are our Mother coming down.

Within Thy gates, Jerusalem, the city called

"The Heavenly"

You are the "Many-Breasted One",

Hope's 'diamond' faceted with Light.

Your many faces shine on us.

And in 'the many', we find One.

You are the One

In all, through all, fulfilling all

And Your Desire is to be known

And, with You, all the Earth, be one.

"Rise up My fair one, come away.

I cannot tell you now from Me

For you are Mine and I Am yours

By marriage, made in Heaven, planned

By Faith in which I frame you, Mine."

10.

My hidden One, Unseen, be found

To be no more "The Unknown God".

Be found and come abide "in" me;

Be here in every way adored.

And, here, let Your face be revealed

And let me hear Your Voice in song.

Let me give voice to what I hear.

"Be not distracted by 'the world'

Or all its ways apart from Mine;

Its litt le foxes spoil the vine."

The lilies of the valley call,

Oh come delight in me, my Lord.

We wait here, open, with the dawn.

The day is yet cool; come to us.

The shadows, to Your coming, go.

Be found in me, within our midst;

Come quickly, Lord.

"Quickly, I come.

Return and show yourself to be

As a gazelle

That grazes on My sheltered slopes.

The hills are Mine; My breast is yours.

I Am the Mountain of I AM;

Among My hills, find cinnamon."

11.

Night after night, upon my bed

I sought You as my True Love is,

Our "first love" was

And is to come.

There, I, abandoned, in Your arms

Have found my name

Engraved upon Your palms in lines

And of such sweet remembrance, read

Of "Israel", I am "The LORD's"

And of, "Remember Me":

"Do this is memory of Me".

I said, "I do".

I am entwined and married to the Vine I AM;

I take You at Your Word, my LORD

With More to be revealed and known.

12.

"Just ask of Me, And I will show you More to come.

Continue on, remembering;

It's in the DNA we share, Life in the Blood,

"Life from the dead, to all the world...

As Rumi ruminated Love.

Mejnun had Leila; you have Me

And in such times as this, I, you.

Keep turning in Return to Me.

Keep coming up, remembering;

Look in the mirror of My Word.

Remember Me; remember Mine.

My Name is yours; take Mine to heart

And plant it there, In marriage to "the land",

To serve.

We are betrothed, in Blood, to be

The Mystery of I AM, "with" you.

Your Maker is your Husbandman.
There is no other but I AM,

The One and Only God there is.

The LORD is One; My Name is One.

You taste a Foretaste of More Love,

Of that which is to come, a Feast,

A Feast of Feasts, a Song of Songs.
That Day, though not yet here, will come.
Such Days of Heaven, come to Earth
With Healing in My wings and rays.
I heard your cries, And have come down
To gather you, unto Myself."

13.

The petals that I follow here
Are from the Thirteen-Petaled Rose,
Beginning with, to End with
LOVE.
Your rainbow banner, LOVE, streams out.
Beneath Your wing I am 'imprinted' by I AM.
I have not been this way before.
Night after night, day after day
I long for You;
I seek but find You not "with" me
In all the ways of my desire,
In ways that I have known before.
You have become
Now always, though "the same"
Yet MORE.
I thirst not, yet I thirst for More.
Love's petals mark the path I seek.
For More, I am
Lovesick
For You.

14.

I called, heard not.

I sought, found not.

I asked but, "No" was the reply

To questions, "Have you seen my Love?"

Then scarcely had I turned away

In such despair that You were gone

That there You were!

That here You are!

That I, upon Your arm, arise

And sing of such Return with Joy:

Come, go with me; come, take me there

To find the room that is prepared.

We enter in

To where I was, myself, conceived

Within that place prepared by You.

I would be pregnant with such Love

As strong as death is strong

Yet More -

Prepared by You to "Go, speak Life!"

At the Command

Of I AM THAT I AM, my LORD.

My Father, Yours,

My heart is open to Your Seed.

The "child" is Father to this man;

I pray You take me in Your arms.

Held in Your hand

Within Your Heart

I pray You plant Yourself in me.

I pray You will o'ershadow me

And come, abide in me, for Good.

For always, Lord, I pray I may abide in You,

The Mystery, "Christ", "in" me, my HOPE.

Your entrance CHANGES EVERYTHING,

Clothes me anew, from inside, out

To be as Your Heart has desired,

The inner and the outer, one;

The Unseen in the seen, revealed.

With You, MORE always comes in Truth.

In deed, You set me free to Live.

15.

I charge you now, with this, and More -

"Awaken love for it is time!

Swing wide your everlasting doors!

Lift up your heads, ye ancient gates!

The King of Glory would come in,

Would "be come into" who you are;

You now are ready

For "More Love"

To shake you to your very core.

You are the apple of His eye."

Who is this King?

Mighty in batt le, seeking to save You

For Himself.

I have not been this way before.

Who is this speaking? Is it I?

As it is writt en, so it is:

It is not I, but Christ in me,

One greater than King Solomon.

You found me in the Wilderness

Within the deserts of such sin

As has corrupted all mankind

That I, despairing, lost all Hope.

My Hope had died.

"Against all hope", I yet believed, cried out.

You came.

You drew me to Yourself; I lived.

16.

You opened up our graves and called.

You put Your 'Peace Rose' in my hand.

Its petals strew my path today.

Such drops of Your Blood mark my way.

Your Blood has marked my blood as Yours.

I am "Korban", a very "living sacrifice".

Nations and tribes are in my blood

And on my tongue:

Through You, I am infused with Life

With Life upon my tongue to speak

And, in abundance, give the Gift

Spread far and wide

From 'Center-point', the Temple that You are to us,

The House of Prayer

Within Thy walls Jerusalem

Unto the ends of all Your Earth.

I meditate on RUMI-nations far and wide

To gather in the souls thus drawn.

I Ruminate on all I find

Cast up upon this narrow strand....

In broken shells and broken dreams

Is wondrous beauty

Seldom seen.

But You, Lord, see the pearls in each.

17.

What's written in the 'sands of time',

The desert sands

Where land meets sky,

Where both meet sighings of the sea?

An S.O.S?

A 'Save Our Souls'?

A 'Song of Songs'?

It's 'All of the above',

And "More" -

"Of Love Unbound"

The Sound of God's Word bathing us,

Washed in the Waters of His Voice.

How can it be?

In Answer to the Grief we bear

Love comes in Waves.

Incoming.

Shaking me awake

To sweep us off our feet

With More.

Love's Presence fills my world with Joy.

May all that I have

Be your own.

May Jesus heal our lives through Love,

Gift us with Peace.

Faith works through Love,

The Substance hoped for

Yet not seen.

18.

Bestowed with robe and signet ring

You carry us; You bring me Home again, to You.

I 'come up' in Your arms again

Trailing the scent of smoking myrrh,

Of frankincense.

A Cloud by day, the Pillar of Your Fire is here,

Accompanies me

As I do, You.

Your Banner over us is LOVE.

Love scents my path

With Wisdom as was Solomon's -

But Greater Wisdom,

Love that's You,

Your Spirit with us

"Through It All".

It's You

It's You

It's You

It's You

And not a thousand foreign loves

With "foreign gods" tagging along.

It's only You,

None else but You

The All-in-all of everything

That was or is

Or will be standing by the Word.

There's More to I AM than we've known.

You are my More.

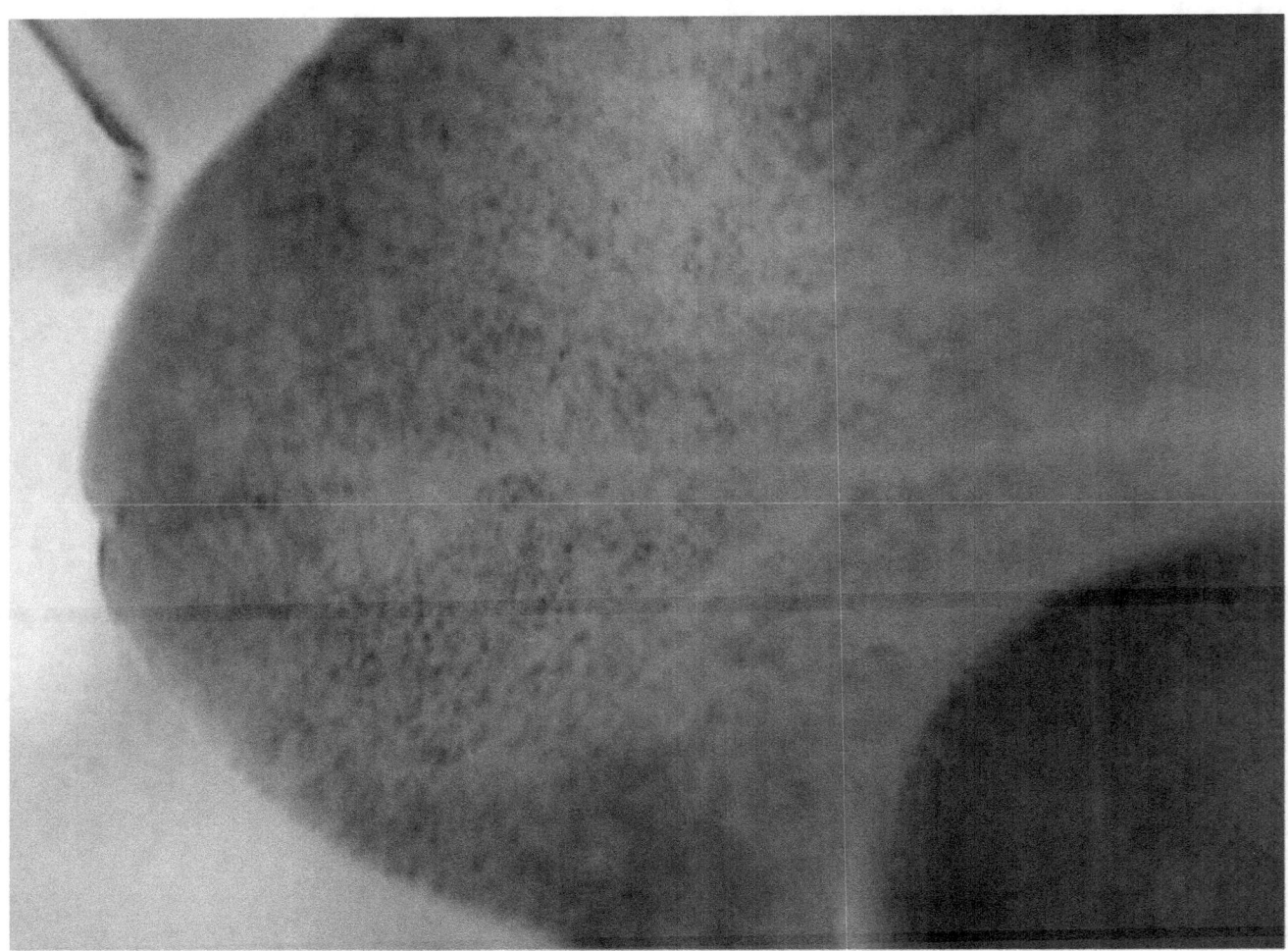

19.

You arm me with an Escort, Lord,
Of warrior angels
Skilled and trained
To deal with demons of the night,
As Darkness spreads across the
Earth. Who can survive?
All those who call upon Your
Name. As Scripture asks,
"What is His Name and His Son's
name If you have known?"
God's Name is One.
The LORD is One.
If God be God, then follow Him.
God sends His Word to heal the
land. There is a Balm in Gilead.
There are yet Miracles to come.

20.

Daughters of Zion, come, come out

And let your Welcome be your love.

Awaken love.

On this His Wedding Day of Joy,

Come and be married to I AM,

And as "the land" and to "the land of Promises",

The Promised land,

Be open, yielding: "Kiss the Son".

Receive the Seed of The I AM:

"Be satisfied within

My arms That, everlasting, carry you."

21.

Such meditations on, about

The Song of Songs I sing to you -

How do I find you?

Beautiful.

Too wonderful to comprehend.

The Fire within these bones is Love.

Your eyes, like doves, coo

Calling me, "Come, lift the veil",

Yet haunt me like the Holy Ghost

Extending everlasting arms.

I, captured, by your hair

Stream down

Like flocks that stream down mountain slopes

To graze in new green grass so sweet

Beside still waters, in Love's grip.

You draw me close.

Your teeth are shining, clean and white.

Fresh as the honey on your lips

Dripping from tasting of the comb,

Your lips like parted crimson cords

Have drawn me to sweet whispers, "Come".

Like ripe fruit, opened, they say, "Come.

Partake of me," spilling their Seed

Of "Taste and see"

That I Am with you, for you, here."

In you I find the Mystery of the Christ, revealed.

God's arm encircles me with you.

I lift my eyes to take you in.

Your neck is like a pausing fawn's,

Above me rising up and over

Shadowing the breasts of hills

Of home found on your breast

Whereon I now would lay my head,

Here grazing to my heart's delight

To rise and enter into More.

To rise and go

To mountains of the Myrrh of love,

The hill of Frankincense and Joy.

You are so beautiful, my love.

22.

"Come with me now, from Lebanon.

There, from Isaiah's Tomb, arise

To go forth quickened and renewed.

Down from the heights of lions' dens.

Down from the haunts of leopards' stealth,

Free from the bondage, Fear of Death,

From fear of men

To follow Me

Into the Way of Love I AM.

To valleys where the streams run sweet

In deep and clear pools of your eyes

Reflecting Who I Am "in you".

I overshadow who you are.

Your eyes have captured Mine, My love.

I seek for lovers, finding you Seeking for Me."

23.

You, Lord, my Shepherd and my King,

Oh Husbandman of all that is,

Oh Lover of the souls You form,

Breathe more Life into us, I pray.

Into the depths of Love, I plunge

To swim in Your eyes, pools of Joy.

I know that I have brought You pain,

Have caused You sorrows, called forth tears.

Their rivulets I lick away.

The taste of salt is on my tongue

In Covenant of Marriage made in Heaven, drip

Such tears of Grief and Joy, co-joined, conjoined like twins,

Co-laborers of Life in You,

With You in me and me in You

Becoming one.

Thus I return, repenting, mind changed

For the Good.

My ways and thoughts have not been Yours.

The taste of salt, of Covenant, is on my tongue.

My heart is Yours.

Keep me to be

The very apple of Your eye.

24.

My heart is Yours.

You've stolen it with one eye closed,

The other framing me with Faith.

You choose to see me as You do

To give me latitude to change.

Your tears ignite my soul with Love.

With both eyes open, flood my soul

With new ways to see all You are.

I am no more the man I knew;

The man I once was now is gone;

A "new creation" takes his place

To be, as You are, with me, now,

An inner, spirit-man, of Faith,

The "substance" of those "born of God".

25.

You have not left me all alone.

Your prayer that we be one, is so.

One with the maid 'from Lebanon',

we have become the Bride of Christ

and You, Beloved, dwell in me.

One with the man 'from Lebanon',

The walls of separation, down

Are gone;

They have been breached.

I have no borders but I AM

For You are "with" me where we go.

You send me as You once were sent.

Can eye not see

As deep and high

As wide as Your arms stretched can be

The Sign of Everlasting Love, of Peace

Of Your "arm" that has been "revealed"

To rescue souls found perishing?

Who has believed? Hineni, LORD.

I have believed.

Your arm becomes my Harbor's arm,

The Haven sought.

You are my Shelter through the storm,

My Shield and very great Reward.

26.

I have been married to the land,

To people of the LORD, I AM,

And have become a "bride of Christ"

Under the Bell called "Liberty".

Let Freedom ring

Throughout the land

To all inhabitants thereof.

Amen.

27.

I am, in Him, now one with Her,

Our Mother coming down to Earth,

The City sought by Abraham.

The Father in Him is in me

Where I am, with Him, one with you.

Formed in the womb, umbilicaled,

Formed in our Mother, Peace, comes down

To be, within your walls, revealed

As "New Jerusalem" descends.

What's up?

Let those with ears to hear-

"Shalom, Salaam and, Peace to all

Who enter in the Arms of Love."

Who has believed?

Our labor is to yet do so, to "hear and do"

Outside the walls of all traditions, true and false,

To find Provision of Your "More".

28.

"Let there be MORE!" still rings within my ears

And calls.

All souls fall short of Who You Are.

All need the Help within Your arm

To be thus carried into Love,

Borne by the Spirit of I AM.

Let God be True

For men have lied.

Men only prophesy "in part" Of all that is the More-to-come.

Apart from Your Word, ours fall short.

By Your Word I both live and die,

Rise from the ashes,

Spread my wings,

Soar on my passion

Just for You.

I find You everywhere I look;

From here, there, even in the midst of hell, The many hells on Earth, to be

As close as calling on Your Name...

The unseen Substance of our Faith.

I keep on calling on

Your Name;

Your Presence is required to live.

29.

Beneath the surface of the seen

Your Love became my Guardian

Becomes "the same", always the same.

Forsaken not, with me, You are

The HOPE that CHANGES EVERYTHING.

You have me covered, front and back,

Coming and going,

Words that spell it out, my shirt.

My daughters keep me well supplied:

Hope Changes Everything: Love Wins

Under Your wing,

Your Love awakens love in them.

At Your Desire, let there be More.

Sweet Love becomes my Guardian,

With one eye always open

Keeps

Against all evil

All who come

To be the apple of Your eye.

30.

Though Love has slain me, yet I live.

Though laid low, yet I rise again.

Thought spent by Love, renewed to shine

With strength of youth restored to last

Until I am at last "no more"

And pass, unseen, across the threshold,

Through the Door.

I hear You knocking on my heart.

I rise to take in all You are.

Both Life and Death are on Your tongue

And though You slay me

Love will win.

31.

I, in the valley of the plain

Am lifted, borne on eagle wings

Lift up my eyes

Take in and taken by surprise, expire

Here on the heights

Beneath the shadow of Your breasts

As snow-capped mountains stand erect

And stream with such Delight in Love

That I am no more who I was.

Changed in the twinkling of an eye

Now I am Yours

And You are mine.

32.

There are no boundaries where I am.

We have become and are as one.

How beautiful you are my bride.

And how long has it been, untold

Throughout the ages was and is

Ancient of days

That I AM longed to take us in His arms again. As I

long, taking you in mine, to sing

And have you wrap me in your limbs

Entwining me, embraced, encircled with your scent

Oh blossomed planting of I AM.

In my heart, God has planted you

To scent this Eden

Sweet with love.

Your touch, the touch of me in you,

Bears fruit.

Ripened and crushed

The grapes of our love make me drunk

On Wine of the Beloved

Comes

In streams found More

Than I had dreamed as possible.

You, love, as mine

Have now become a honeycomb.

The sting of love, the piercing of it

Now forgotten in your arms,

The rending has re-membered me. We are made

whole as one, restored.

33.

The sting of love

Is washed away

By streams that make me Glad

In you.

The piercing, sealed,

Your lips drip sweetness, nectar, honey

Oil and wine that heals my wounds.

The more I taste

The more I see

Of more than I had ever dreamed

Could be.

Love had been veiled

But now awake

Within this 'lucid dream', I dream

The very "Magnum Dream" of You.

34.

Lest I be blinded by Your Light

I see but darkly, through a glass

The Mystery of the Christ "in you"

Who sees in me "the same" revealed

Through eyes of faith

To be a "husbandman" to Yours.

To be a "bride of Christ" to You

As wife within a rib, a door.

After Your image we are made.

Formed of the dust

And Breathed upon

Becoming More, in Love, than loss.

Becoming Gain

For "Christ in you"

Is Great Reward,

The Shield of Father Abraham.

Before him, You were Word with God,

To be the Lord-with-us on Earth.

 In You we are in

Love with Him.

The LORD is He Who takes us in.

Whose is the Dream

And who, the dreamer of such things?

It's all of the above, in You.

I find it so, that You, the All-in-all Are here.

35.

I take you in

And you take me.

As breasts express

The milk of human kindness

Flows

With miracles made flesh through Word

In babes thus rocked

And held, thus cradled, in Your arms -

Love wins.

It's Mother's Day;

I'm thanking You

For all the Kindness of I AM.

The Milk of Your Love

Makes us strong.

We can grow up, to break such Bread

And to partake

Of Water turned to Wine

You pour

Of the Beloved

In my heart

And on my tongue.

Salvation is not far away.

36.

As breasts express the milk of miracles made flesh

To infants in Your Kingdom come,
To new-born, second born, thus birthed,

So too

On our tongues

From these lips

Comes Mystery

In the form of Love

Of Word made flesh

Like seed expressed

To penetrate the egg

And live.

Like seed expressed to nurture hope

So have the Words I speak

Been sent.

I taste and see

The Word I speak of God is Love.

You have become

The garden into which I sow.

I plant in you the honeyed scents

Of More-to-come.

Will you get pregnant

As I am, with Word of God,

The Mystery of what is revealed?

I pray in this we may be one.

37.

Your clothes bear scents of Lebanon

Of cedars that shall build His House,

The "House of Prayer"
That all the nations may come up, and celebrate

The Coming of the One with us

That, through, from Sorrows

Joy comes forth.

If we walk in the Flame of Love

Its Tongues shall bathe us

In His Peace,

A Peace that is not

Of the world

But of the Kingdom

Sought and found.

What once was Loss

Shall be great Gain.

Deserts shall fill

With pools again

And streams shall overflow

Our tongues.

From our lips

Shall such Honey

Drip.

38.

Your cheeks, like slopes,
Grow into orchards of such fruits
Of every incense bearing tree.
A garden of the Lord's Delight,
Your garden opens up to me.
In mounds I leave the Seed of Song.
In you I run
In streams of sheer delight, arise As
fountains are released
Spring up
To overfl ow the banks.
Flooded we are with Wealth untold
But not of silver or of gold
Give I to you
Such as I have
Of Word deposited
Of Him.
God calls us to be one in Love; Such
as I have, I give to you. Freely I
give as I receive
For you are mine
And I am yours
We of one body and one fl esh And
born to be
Of One Blood, His,
The sons and daughters of I AM
Led by The Spirit
Into More.

39.

The honeyed moon

In witness drips

Over Jerusalem of gold

Its light

Refl ected from the Sun Who comes

Arises over us with Joy

With Healing in the wings and rays

That bathes the city's stones

And hearts.

Our bodies tremble with such Joy. We

are released from fear by faith;

"Only believe, fear not" You said.

"No longer are you lambs from birth,

Or deaf and dumb

Or found to be untouchables.

For I Am yours and you are Mine As

New Creations born above

To be entwined

As one within

The Garden of Love's sweet delight,

The Vineyard of the King of kings.

This is the Treasure kings have sought

And beggars at the gate have found.

Your body leaps and shouts with Joy.

In Me, such Books, of Acts

Await.

Wait on the LORD

To fi nd Me while I may be found."

40.

The chapter, five; the verse is one.

This is the Grace of God, with us:

Drunk on the Wine

Of the Beloved

Found in you

To be a fountain

Opened up,

I in the flow of love am drunk,

Carried away

Beside myself

In your embrace.

With "Joy unspeakable"

I step

Into the More of You to come.

I lean upon "The Unknown God",

Not on Your tomb, but on Your arm,

And by Your Word

Make EXIT from the Wilderness.

41.

I come forth, staggered,
Wounded
Not alone
Found leaning on the Arm of Love,
Your "arm" fulfilling all the Law
And all the prophets
Found as One
In Word thus sent
To, "Love the LORD
With all your heart and mind and strength.
And love your neighbor as yourself."
In this, I am stripped bare and clothed.
Renewed I am, to come forth
Leaning
On Your arm,
That of The Unseen
To be known.
I bear such witness on my tongue.
The Kingdom comes
In me to be
The Word made flesh
Of Christ in you...
The Mystery of the One Who comes
First in a cloud
"the size of one man's hand"
Here cupped
To pour out all I have
Received.

42.

I do this freely, not of me

But, "by My Spirit, says the LORD,

The same that raised Christ from the dead.

If that same Spirit dwells in you

Then may you do the same and More.

For More Love has been poured on you

In better Covenant with Me."

I cup, to pour out what I have

On you, in you, through you, to be

The MORE that I have sought to find.

I have been on an Odyssey.

A way was opened "through the sea".

My soul is on her Vision Quest

To make Love plain

And "run with it".

To cross the "Finish Line" With Joy.

I am His Joy

And you are mine,

The city of my chief delight.

Jerusalem.

In you, a Fountain opens up.

43.

Spring up O well

A spring of crystal clear and sweet

The Water in you is alive.

It rises, drips

A fountain sealed

Uncorked, explodes

In New Wine raining down

With More.

It pours from heights of Lebanon,

Streams down Mount Hermon's slopes and pools.

I find in You I am immersed

In springs of Living Water, sweet.

Thus am I scented by I AM;
Some say it's Life,

Some call it Death.

Some hurry closer, drawn by You.

Some flee as if the life they choose

Is to be lived

Without Your Name.

North Wind, awake!

South Wind, awake!

Call all souls from the East and West.

Gather the exiles; Breathe on these.

Can these bones live?

Come Breathe on me.

44.

Blow on my garden; 'waken love.

Awaken love

That Love's perfume may swallow me,

That my Beloved may come down,

May hear my cries

And be come back to Israel,

To "be come in", with Fullness shared

To taste of its rare fruits, in you.

I have been satisfied by God

On honey, Wine, on milk, and More.

I have enough to share with you.

Life without end now overflows.

Come and partake.

Come eat and drink.

Pay with admission on the tongue.

Pay with your lips and "kiss the Son",

The only Debt remaining, Love.

Outstanding is the Taste of More.

Come and partake

Until you too are drunk on Love

On Wine of the Beloved, poured.

I have received that I may share;

I share that I may yet receive

A Double-Portion of I AM,

The Second Coming of my Lord,

45.

The Lover of my soul is here.

For Love, I am stripped bare and wait,

Await His coming like a bride, a "wife of youth"

Beloved of I AM

Restored in radiance to shine,

Arise to shine

Found open to

The "Let there be More!"

On His tongue.

I know that my Redeemer lives.

I stand still, praising, waiting

Sure.

"Your life, a prayer, requires that you

Continue on, continue on;

Do not shrink back to be destroyed.

Fear not, Oh My beloved; sing.

Only believe, fear not, and sing.

Our notes meet in the air, form rain

The smell of which is sweet to Me,

Sweet to My ear, its falling is.

So, sing the night away

Till Dawn

For I AM coming

On the clouds."

46.

I sleep and yet my heart is not;

It sings upon my bed, awake,

With 'one eye open' looks for you;

It is 'all ears'

To catch the sound of Your sweet, Yes.

Of, "Yes, I come"

In singing over me in song,

My dry soul wet

With Morning's Dew.

You drop down and You smell like Rain.

You hover over us with Love.

Your feathers hide us in Your arms.

Oh my Beloved, come again.

Come, roar in on Your "tongues of fire"

And lick away the caul of my New Birth in You,

Lick up the water that is poured

Upon this "Korban", sacrifice.

I give You all my praise and More.

I seek to give You all my love.

You see my 'little' as much More.

You turn my water into Wine.

I am 'all ears'

To catch the whispers of Your Love,

To hear the sound

Of "one hand clapping"... "Here AM I",

Announcing that The Spirit moves,

Is manifest, in Word-made-flesh.

47.

I hear You knocking at my door.

Your footsteps tremble me with More.

The Promise of Your Coming, lives.

It lives in me.

I tremble at Your coming, Lord.

I lift my head and lift my eyes

To enter in

The Door that opens in Your side.

You take us as Your Eve once was

To be the Bride of Christ You are

Who formed us in Your image, "Mine",

To take the image of my Lord's.

The Second Adam of I AM,

The Gardener of all things new

Of "All Things Bright and Wonderful".

You are "too wonderful" for me

To comprehend

Your Love is mine.

The ring hung from my neck says so.

The three rings hung there

Say so much.

I cannot comprehend it all.

Your Love is deeper than I am.

I am immersed.

I breathe in Water, yet I live.

I kiss Your face and I arise.

I sit here dripping wet and wait.

48.

A Window opens over us.

With echoes of your '48,

The year of my Rebirth has come.

Here in the twinkling of a star

The banner of your flag unfurls.

Here in the twinkling of an eye,

The twinkling of a tear, a sign,

The apple of Your eye awakes

To take us in

"Just as I Am"

To be as "signs in Israel".

Here in an instant, suddenly,

Within Your face, within a Window, in a Door,

Within You, I am changed to be

More like You than I was before.

The man I once was is "no more".

I prophesy of days to come:

The days of More-to-come, Unfold

Like Blossoms of Your Love that buds

On us as "sticks snatched from the fire".

To live again as Aaron's rod.

As Moses, in the Hand of God.

"What's in your hand?

The Life I give you in My Name.

To spend upon the Debt of Love.

For this, you have been Born Again;

Comfort My people, says your God."

49.

Oh taste and see

Of what I speak

That drips with honey

Golden, sweet

Glazed from the "tongues"

That capture us

To burn away the taste of loss

And set us free

To speak of You

That Love may enter

Into these, in you, in me

As Mystery, "Christ"

GOD's Word

"Made flesh"

To be in us

The Form to follow

Into More.

Both male and female

Formed He, us

To be thus married to His Word

Ecstatic, trembling, satisfied.

To, "thirst no more".

Found dancing through the night

To come.

What of the night?

Watchman, the Dawn!

50.

Fifty, set free, debt free.

All debt is cancelled but Love's Debt

Too great to pay

But not to 'live out', day by day,

Redeeming what remains

Of Time.

"So, come again.

Open to Me

My sister, dearest, perfect dove

Who seeks the cleft within the Rock,

Within the Mountain's side I AM...

To enter you

As, "Alice through the looking glass"

Who sees into an unseen world.

What Realm is that?

My Kingdom come.

My Kingdom comes unseen in you.

My head is wet.

My palms are cupped

Your name therein

Drenched with the dripping Dew of Dawn,

My hair, with lucid dreams

Of Love.

Come, take with Me the Wings of Dawn

And let us fly away to More."

51.

When my Beloved

Slipped God's hand,

God's fingers like "the Keys", inside,

Of "Kingdom come", unseen "in you",

The latch-hole of my waiting heart,

My inmost being,

Trembling

Stirred.

When I arose

And cried for my Beloved, "Come!",

My hands were dripping with such Myrrh

In streams as run down Hermon's sides.

52.

Spring up, O Fountain, like a well, Artesian in

the heart of us

For all who thirst for More of God.

To find

That God is More, by far,

Than our Traditions have portrayed....

For "all have sinned and fallen short".

Traditions are not Who God Is.

Our words fall short.

Our ways cannot portray the Truth Of the

Unseen, Unspeakable

Except "in part"

Of Who You Are with us

For Good.

Our marriage here is but a sign

Of how You long to be "with" us.

As husbands are with wives, "in" love,

Held precious and as treasure found

To be as "one flesh", here on Earth

So too, You would be found "in" us

To be "as one", as "one new man"

The Second Adam,

We as Eve.

Those born "of God"

And not by our will, but of Yours,

To be all we can be

In Love

Where "nothing is impossible".

53.

I opened up my hands to You,

Thinking to hold You as my own,

To take You to be only Mine,

But Love had turned away and gone. You turned Your back

On such exclusive rights to Truth.

I called You but You did not come.

I sought You but I found You not.

The watchmen met me where I was.

They struck me and they took my robe.

I was undone

With thinking You are only mine.

Oh daughters of Jerusalem,

He comes to you as well as me,

To others at the ends of Earth,

And even to our enemies

With all the Fullness of I AM.

Awaken Love.

Awaken to the Facts of Love,

Be ready to receive of More.

"Let there be MORE!" echoes in me.

To fi ll the void the echoes leave,

I must share all I have, with you.

So, if you find Him, tell Him this,

That I am faint with love,

For More.

54.

Why is He More?

Why is Christ MORE than we have known?

Why should we thus be charged by you

To 'waken love

Found foreign to the way we think?

To be a messenger, of Love

Found foreign to the way we are?

Because He Is

The bright and morning Star,

Of David, of The I AM, sent

To be the Light, the True Light of the Life of men,
The risen Sun of Righteousness,

Of Right Relationship with G D,

The Spirit, LOVE,

The G D Who is Love over us.

His robe has filled the temple with

His Banner over us, unfurled.

His Living Word of Love is this

That, "Mercy triumphs over Wrath".

How is it so?

Because His arms were spread for us

To be The Sacrifice for Sin

And by His wounds our Healing comes

That we may be one in His arms.

His Love will make Man whole again.

Of this, I am a messenger.

55.

Both fair and ruddy is our King,

The Fairest of ten thousand 'gods',

The rest, all false

And built on lies

Or, images, mirages shimmering with hope

Like fingers pointing to the stars

Where, there, the heavens still declare

That Christ alone remains the "Word"

Of "HOPE" that "CHANGES EVERYTHING".

Just ask the birds and animals.

Just ask the bees.

Just ask the Earth.

Just ask the sky.

Just ask the seas.

Breakers arise, form and roll in

To crash and break, here at the foot,

Here at the Face of Christ, the Rock,

The Stone Face of Salvation's wall,

The high cliff, fissured Face of God,

The Face of I AM

With us

In a Heart of Flesh,

The Risen One

Who came to show us what Love is.

Love Wins.

Oh seas of all humanity, wash in your mist of roaring waves

The feet of Him Who seeks to save.

Wash with your tears, the feet of Love.

How Blessed be the feet of Him Who brings Good News

And freely offers Love, to us.

Oh seas of a humanity

Laid waste by sin

Bathe in your mist

The Brow of Love.

I would that I might sing of the unspeakable

Full of the Joy, the Glory of I AM, of Strength,

Of Love found Stronger than all fear

"Mighty to save"

And conquer Death.

I would that I might sing of this and have you hear

The Lover that is sent to us

To follow through the lives we live -

Redeemer, Savior, Signs to follow Words He speaks.

I would that I might comfort you

With all with which He comforts me - With Love.

And that we might arise, as one

To be no more as we have been,

But, risen, shine.

For this is Love - that we be "crucified with Christ",

Our hearts found circumcised by God

To rise and shine as "one new man"

From every nation, tongue and tribe.

56.

Surrounded as Love is

With Light,

His lifting face will shine and make

Jerusalem "of gold" again,

The finest gold.

Armed with the Purity of Love,

Of Dawn that is the

Light of Life

His Face will come and shine on us.

The Truth will come and dawn on us

To look upon the

One we pierced.

57.

Your hair, like feathers, whispering

Is singing over us with Peace.

Like palm fronds over pools

You Breathe

And stir the surface of the soul

To depths

That have not been so stirred

Before.

We have been waiting for Your eyes

To rest on eye pools, mirroring, reflecting there

And in our eyes

The eyes of doves.

You sing to dry our tears of Grief.

"Come unto Me," You call to us,

"and let me wash your loss away."

To gain the I AM, with us

Here.

"I hear your cries and have come down

Immersing you, to baptize you

With Fire

In Love

To come forth dripping

Tongues of fire."

Such Love is simple

Simply, "beyond words".

58.

I sit before your feet, am drawn

To tell the story of such Love.

To spring up now, with streams found sweet

From wells of such Salvation dug

To sprinkle you with what I drink.

I pour out what is poured on me.

Can only give what I receive.

Can only speak of what I sense.

Can only point to what I see.

I pray you get a taste

For "More"

That your joy may be also,

"Full".

59.

Come, rest your head

Upon the Breast

Of God, the Many-Breasted-One,

The All-Sufficient One Who Is

The Father/Mother of all things,

Our Peace.

We, in 'His image' have been made

Both "male and female"

To make Love

And to "be fruitful",

Multiply.

Let there be More.

In marriage, 'made in Heaven', planned We are reflections of His Love.

G_D's lips drip liquid Myrrh

On us.

His hands rain wonders down on

Earth. With Healing in

His wings and rays,

His Touch works miracles in hearts.

He wounds to heal

And slays to raise us up again.

The Rod of God's Love opens us,

Parts seas that roar

To enter into Covenant,

To open up the ancient Way

Made New through Resurrection Life:

"To be that which I AM, in you".

60.

His fingers, dripping Life and More,

Are like God's Keys that enter us

Probing old wounds

To open up

The Way into

The Covenant

Remaining "New"

In Jeremiah thirty-one.

His belly, like a tablet, carved,

Reads like the "Love" of God for man,

Says, "I AM, pregnant, with your lives.

You must be 'born again', of God."

His aspect is like Lebanon, its cedars hewn

To form the Temple of thy God;

Given, He rose, in three days time.

He overshadows lives with Love,

Rejoicing over us, in song.

His whispers are Desirable.

Listen to me, Oh daughters of Jerusalem.

Oh where has your Beloved gone?

61.

Oh where has your

Beloved gone?

Which is the Way

HE may be found? Which is the Way

SHE may be known?

We have not known

God as God Is And as

His arm has been revealed.

I come with

Good News; who believes?

Who has believed and will believe

The Good Report that we bring back

From seeking to the ends of

Earth The Love the nations have desired.

Who is this One called their

"Desire"? Here, take my hand;

Together we may seek His face.

Down to His vineyard, He has come And will return

Seeking for Eden, in our hearts.

He hears my cries, and has come down

To find us seeking after Him,

Down to find gardens in our hearts

Of Longing, in Remembrance of

The Garden where God walked with man.

Where in the evening's cool, we talked.

62.

Drawn to Love's vineyard, Love has come

To find in our hearts

Room for More

To find a place prepared for Him

In beds of such Delight as knows

That, 'I am His and He is mine'.

His is The Dew upon the vine,

The Sweetness in the open bud.

The open flower in the field,

The Pearl of such great value found

In shells of lives

Found broken at the feet of God.

"Ripe unto harvest", we are His

As "the Beloved" has been mine.

I pray that you partake of this,

Can taste and see

Of Mystery found

In "Christ in you".

Such HOPE still CHANGES EVERYTHING.

In you God seeks such sweet delight.

"How long I've sought to gather you..."

This is the Word of God to man.

Christ would be found

Is waiting to be sought and ask,

"Would You be mine?"

63.

His whispers are desirable,

Like palm fronds over pools,

Like wings,

Like doves,

Like eyes announcing Depths of Love,

As God desires to be "with" us,

So Word, in you, desires to be

The open Mystery of The Book,

The arm of the Unseen, revealed,

God's reach into our Grief, with Joy.

He gave Himself

To be the Bridegroom of the soul.

Come look upon the Son we pierced,

The Lion-Hearted, "King of kings".

When you do this

His eyes will only be for you.

You are the apple of His eye.

He sees by faith, the Substance He Desires "in you".

So, by faith, step into His arms,

Across this Threshold, into More

And, lift the veil
To, "kiss the Son".

This is God's sweet, express Desire.

I stand in witness: There is More.

Choose Life and live,

In the Abundant Love of God.

Where Mercy triumphs over Wrath.

64.

I speak to you, of things that He desires to say.

"What is His Name and His Son's Name?"

Always the same and always one,

The Truth, Beloved, of I AM.

"You are," He says,

"You are," the Spirit whispers here,

"As lovely as Jerusalem,

As beautiful a bride as is My "wife of youth"

Restored to be, Forever, More, With Me, again,

Prepared and ready for the Feast.

Let it begin, with "first love", here, remembered, sweet.

By faith, you taste and see the Truth."

The Fire in your eyes, dazzles Me

"For this, I formed you in the womb

Within My walls, Salvation's arms, Jerusalem's

Of She, your Mother, coming down.

She comes down from above on wings;

On clouds, She bears Me, found "in you".

The Spirit and the bride are one.

Both speak 'the language' of My tongue

Upon which Life and Death abound.

Where Mercy triumphs, over Wrath.

For this I formed you in the womb,

To be drawn close, to grow up and awaken love

And then to "Kiss the Son" I AM."

65.

"What is My Name?

My Name is Spirit, spilled as Love,

Spelled out and spoken as My Word

That you may hold upon your tongue

As Bread from Heaven, sent to break

And make you whole

For this I formed you in the womb,

To be Mine that I may be yours.

Your parted lips hold seeds of love

That I inhabit in your praise.

I live within the songs you sing.

I hear your cries and have come down

To be your All-in-all, the One.

You are the apple of My eye;

My eyes are now for you alone.

Re-membered with My body parts,

Though they be many, I AM One.

My eyes hold promises of More

As if there were no other doves

But you who come to light on Me.

The Dawn of your Awakened Love

Bears witness as a moon that's full,

Her soft light spilling over seas,

Majestic as the stars above.

How many are you, as the stars?

I see as many as will come."

66.

I do not know myself in this;

It is too wonderful for me.

I am undone.

I am a man of unclean lips

Appearing now in rags to be

Among a people of the same.

I pray You come, clothe us anew

In Who You Are....

I think I shall go hide myself.

I am not worthy, Lord, of More.

I tremble in my inmost parts.

If I see More, I think that I shall die of Love.

Lovesickness makes me weak

For You.

67.

"Come back, come back, Oh Shulammite

That We may gaze on you as Ours

To be a "bride of Christ", as formed,

"both male and female", formed as Ours

Once planted in an Eden, lost.

Return and be restored through Word,

The Word that I AM, sent to heal,

That, by My Spirit, makes you whole.

By Word that I AM, with you, now.

Who will believe?

Oh come and dance with Me again

As in the dance of Mahanaim,

Of two hosts, male and female, one,

A wrestling of war and peace,

Mercy and wrath.

Come kiss the Prince of Peace,

The Son.

Make Peace; be Blessed.

Get pregnant with the Word of G D;

The Missing Link is "Christ in you".

Oh come and dance within My arms.

Come lay Me down, with you, to be

A goblet full of wine I drink.

Your belly, like a field of wheat,

Bordered by lilies where I graze

Is where I long to lay My head."

68.

Your eyes have drawn me into pools

Where I breathe "Living Water", found

To be the Breath of You, my Love.

I breathe You in.

My nostrils flare in sweet surprise

Of Fire that bathes me with Your scent,

The Scent of Life and not of death.

I come out smelling like a rose,

Like You, the Rose of Sharon, smell,

To scent the air, within this world, of Kingdom come

In You Who bring

The first love of my dreams

To pass.

"I Am your Shield and Great Reward.

I AM your Peace, the Haven you have sought, secure.

I give you Me; you give

Me you Till ours becomes one heart on fire,

One body pulsing with such Joy

Of Longing satisfied with More.

My Longing is for you,

My Joy. Yours is for Me.

I hear your cries and have come down."

69.

My Lord, my Longing is for You.

I find You everywhere I turn.

Let us go to Your vineyard, soon

To search for buds

And open blossoms on the vine.

There will I magnify my love.

There will I sing to You of More,

Of all that is unspeakable.

You fill me up to overflow.

And now Streams, from my belly, rise.

The Spirit of You is in me.

70.

"Come to My vineyard; find Me there.

With Treasures found both Old and New,

There will I give to you My Word,

All that I have in store for you -

Hope and a future, Mine to give,

Good and not evil, from My hand.

From Hand-to-mouth, from Heart-to-heart.

From Eye-to-eye, from Me-to-you.

For you to taste and see, and speak."

*****

If only you were born my twin

To so be "born again", again

My brother, sun; my sister, moon

Who suckle at our mother's breasts, "the same"

Within thy gates, again, Jerusalem of Old, renamed

The "New Jerusalem" that comes.

Seated above, I then would take you by the hand

And lead you here to "kiss the Son"

In marriage to the One I AM.

You are to me as my own flesh and blood and bones.

Such Charity begins at home.

Who can despise then, such "More Love"?

There will be those who chasten us,

Who hasten to imprison More;

Some go to great lengths, sent "to save"
To only make of Freedom, "hell".

Count it "but dung", if Liberty in Christ

Is lost.

71.

"The kisses of My mouth are sweet

And, on My tongue, are Life and Death.

My Kiss is Life.

My Touch is Healing to your flesh.

I would "Abide", within your heart

By Faith that is the Substance sought.

Word Is the Substance man requires.

With Love I speak Words over you,

Rejoicing over you in song.

I draw you closer than a friend. I look for lovers, says your God,

A Marriage made in Heaven, planned.

Act out the pattern in the Feast.

I charge you to, "Awaken love".

I rouse you where you once were born;

Again, I bid you,

"Come to Me; And seek Me while I may be found."

Come take Me into you to be

The Seal of Love upon your arm

Revealed to be, Seal of the Prophets,

On your heart,

Engraved therein

To be a sign

Of "I AM With you", always, here,

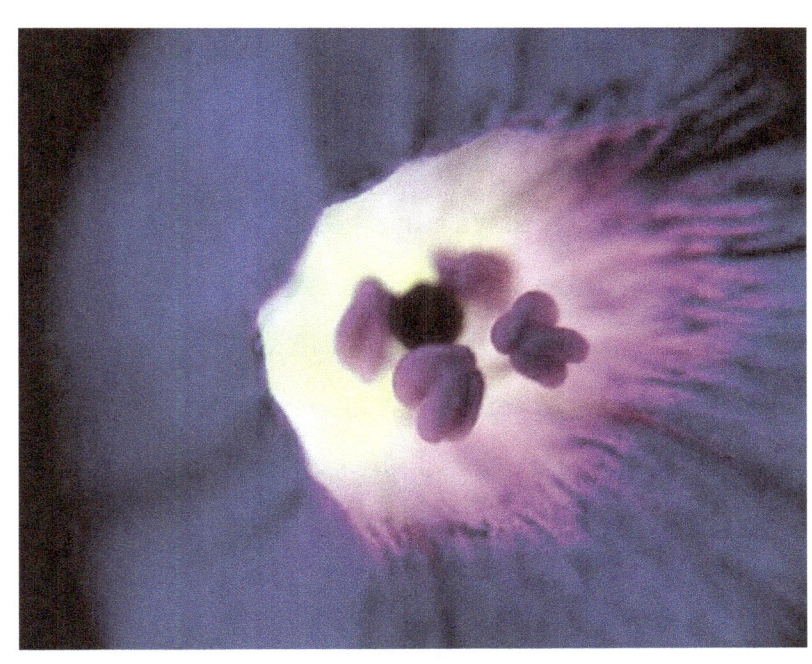

Always the same,

Forever choosing you as Mine.

To "put on Christ", the Star that out of Jacob came,

Wear Me, a Seal, upon your arm.

My Star of David is the Sign

Of Resurrection from the Dead, of Life,

Abundant, MORE-to-come,

Stronger than Death

The last of all your enemies.

I AM your Shield and Great Reward

And what is Mine, I give to you.

My 'Passion', cruel, became a grave

Which, "I AM", opened up to More,

To MORE LOVE Fiercer than the roar

Of flames within the Holocaust.

My Love is Stronger than such Loss;

My Love is Great Gain to the souls

Of Mine, a remnant that survives.

And will again do so to be

"Life from the dead" to all the world.

My roaring over you is Love;

I am the Lion, Judah's King, the Lord of lords,

The Word of God

And many waters quench not Me

Nor My Thirst found for More of you

Nor My Thirst for My Wine in you

To overfl ow the cup I hold

And offer you - to, "Come, be filled!"

No fl ood of water or of fire

Can wash away My Love for you.

No Blood but Mine

Can wash away man's Stain of Sin.

Such 'Washing of the Word' is yours;

I freely give it as a Gift.

Its Value is above all things.

Your heart was formed to hold such Life

As are "the Riches" of the Christ.

For this, I Am, with you, the Source.

For you, I do "provide Myself",

"A ram" once in the thicket caught,

Crowned with the thorns that I once wore.

But Mine now crown Me with the crowns

Of Buds and Blossoms of My Love,

The same wherewith I have crowned them,

The Comfort of My Father, shared.

The Love I Am

Cannot be bought or sold by man.

Nor do I come

For 'love of money', But, for you."

72.

Who do I speak to?

You, I hope.

Some 'older than Methuzlah',

Some older than once Enoch was

When, suddenly, he was "no more".

And others, those not come of age,

Those not here yet,

To brothers yet unborn again,

Uncircumcised of heart and mind

Too young to know Love as it is;

And little sisters with no breasts

Too young to know You as a man.

You are but "Mystery" in their thoughts

And yet the "Unknown God" to them.

What shall we do, when "marriage", to You

'Speaks' to them

To come and "be" the "Bride of Christ"?

Will this confuse them even more?

What shall we say to those who ask?

How can we offer what we have?

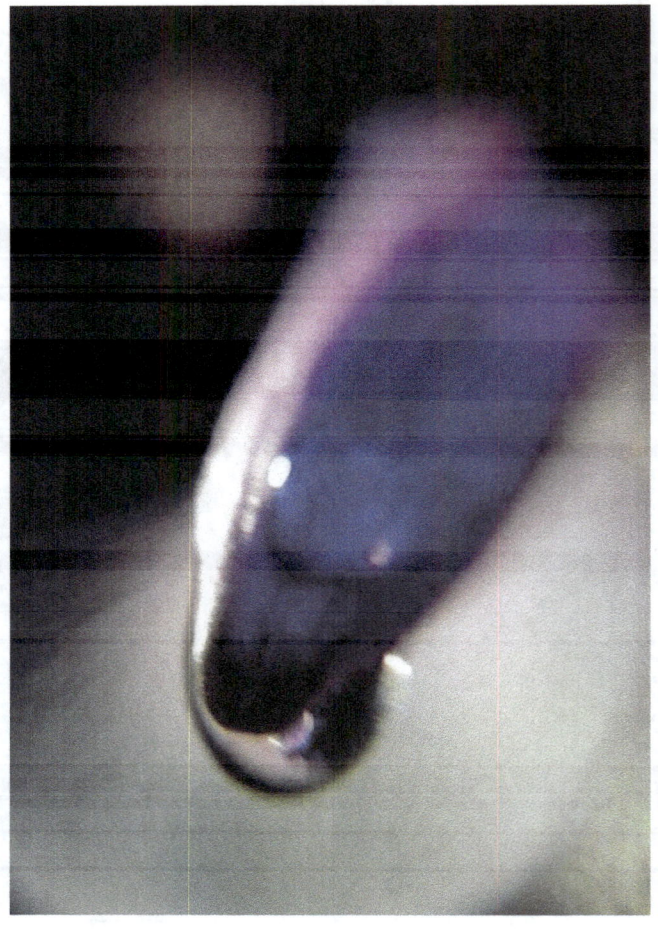

73.

"Permit them all to come to Me

And be immersed, baptized in Fire

And washed in Waters of the Word.

All, "by My Spirit", says the Lord.

Permit them all to come to Me,

Encourage them just as they are,

Just as you are,

Just as I Am

To seek for More,

Both young and old,

Both male and female:

"Kiss the Son":

Be married to the One I AM Found in "the chosen"

"Promised land". And prophesy,

"Come from the four winds To My arm."

74.

Don't be a fool for less than More.

Send out an SOS, to God.

Sing out your own sweet Song of Songs.

And if you have none, ask for More.

Let there be More!

Wisdom of Solomon, arise

And speak to us,

"Awaken Love"

And live Love out

The Greater Love

Of "Christ in you".

"Greater is He", found "with you", now.

Be still and know He is the Lord.

Come, look upon the

Love we pierced. Insert your own hand in

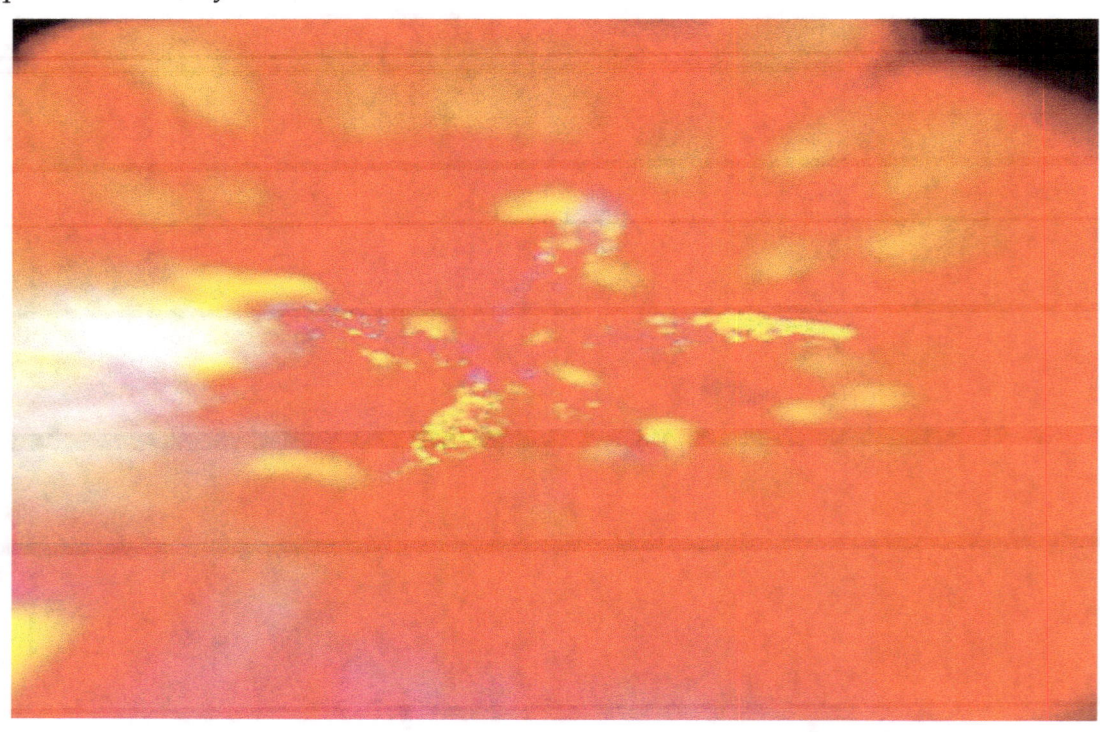

Love's side; It comes out holding

Keys to More.

The Kingdom comes, unseen, in you.

Then shall the Just man take his stand;

His confidence, not of himself, Is found in God.

For some time now

Each just man has not been his own;

Each one, with Words, has Voiced "the same",

Has said as much or more than this:

'It is no longer I that live

But Christ Who lives inside of me.'

What does it mean

When all I seem to face is woe

As darkness spreads to fill the Earth?

"As in the days of Noah", comes.

And I, in Him, Salvation's Ark,

Am found to be

Hidden and Loved,

Will suddenly be found,

Quite unexpectedly,

Home safe,

And counted as a son of God,

Re-membered with God's daughters, one

Given a place prepared for us

Among the chosen of the LORD,

Among His own

And married to the land they saw,

Its City, sought by Abraham.

Men then will see

The wise man's End,

The Purpose God proposed to us

To be, somehow, the Bride of Christ

By simply saying, "Yes. I do."

He was, "consumed with zeal" for us

To be the house that takes Him in

That all "the body" might be one,

"both male and female", in "The Name",

Both married to the One Who comes.

Laughed at in scorn, made fun of as

A madman ending in disgrace,

Outside the camp, cut off, cut down,

Cast down and out,

The butt of the contempt of jokes,

His pearls were trampled in the dust

And He, Himself,

Provided by and for His Ends

There Breathed His last Words, crushed by God,

A target for Rome's pointed jabs,

Hung on a tree, to be "a curse"

Taking our sins upon Himself,

Becoming Poor,

Disguised as but a beggar, stripped

And mocked that some had called him, "King".

Don't be a fool and don't say "No"

To G D, Who sent His Word "to heal"

For "by his wounds" we have been healed.

As it is written, so it is.

He rose to call us once again:

He opens up our graves and cries.

My voice, as but an echo, says,

"Come, follow me;

With great abandon, hear and do

The Word upon my tongue I share -

I call you, come and "kiss the Son"!

Be married to the One He is, I AM with you,

King of the Jews, the Prince of Peace,

Long sought, not found,

The Light of Life, Eternal Flame

Amid the darkness you prefer,

Traditions that enthrone your ways

And your thoughts found divorced from Him.

I burn with His Love just for you.

Ignited, ringing wet, I am

Undone by Fire within my bones.

Come, with me and be soon immersed

In Waters turning to New Wine

Becoming Tongues of Fire that sing

Of the Beloved,

All I need and More, for you.

This I must publish, live and breathe

To be set "free indeed" by Truth

That from my youth

I seek to find.

His Mercies are new, every day.

With Him, come many treasured Pearls;

Sweet is the Wisdom of I AM.

Into Her house, I bid you, Come.

She is our Mother, coming down

To Birth us through the Gates of More.

I bid you, Come and enter in, to Covenant.

Awaken love, to take Christ as your "Husbandman".

The Word, our Maker, has become

The very Lover of our souls

And we, His "wife of youth", now are

Re-membered, to be one, restored

Made in His image, "one new man".

75.

I bid you, Come, stand still and ask.

Stand at the Crossroads, ask and see

Wherein the Good Way, open, waits

To carry us

Across the Threshold

Into More.

Its line I write of in the sand;

I draw a picture with my songs.

I sing us to Him, yet to come

Into the "Fullness" spoken of.

A few say, "Yes!".

But many shrink back from such Love,

From such abandon, fall away

With, "We will not!

With "No!", we are divorced from More;

The Invitation, "Marry Me", is turned to Loss

And great grief grows

Instead of Joy.

It all becomes "unspeakable".

I cannot tarry longer here.

I sense Him calling, "Come away.

As I AM with you, be with Me.

The world is too much with you, child.

Come, enter in the Door I Am;

For you I Am the Way and Life.

There is no other than I AM.

Let there be More

And if you love me, feed my flocks."

76.

Permit them all to come to Me.

As I AM, you become a door.

Permit them all to come through you.

Receiving you, they enter Me

Both young and old,

Those just born and those close to death,

Those with all life ahead of them

And those who have already 'lived'.

offer something wholly new,

The Holy "New Thing" that I do In making all things new again -

The Gift of God, "Eternal Life" Which comes unseen

To give them More of Who I AM, A New Inheritance in Christ,

The Lift that's in My Blood "in you",

The DNA of My "True Vine"

Entwining souls with More to come.

My vineyard is My Israel

The men of which

Must take Me as their "Husbandman"."

Send me to them; or, better yet,

Permit them, Lord, to come to me as "Israel"

To be here, where I am, "with" you.

I bear the "Witness" of Your Name

And to You I will turn their hearts.

"The King's Voice" You have given me.

I once much, like a sailor, cursed,

Was 'Lost at Sea' but now am Found

And now I speak Encouragements,

And Blessing in the Name of God.

And Warning as it comes to me

As once it came to Balaam's ass.

Your Life is on my tongue to speak

Of 'marriage made in Heaven', please;

And no more Funerals, Death, Divorce.

I know Your Name and it speaks volumes of Your

Love. Love tore me down to 'build me up', into

Your House, To be a House of

Prayer for all. In prayer I do "continue on"

And in "submission" am a "stone", living not dead,

"Of Witness/Ed" (verse 34)

As written of in Joshua, the Hebrew Scriptures, KJV,
In Chapter twenty-two, of this....
How can it be?

The Word is Living, always is and always was,
Always will be, "always the same",

The True Light, still, of every man.

And so Word is, to me, as "Ed",

As "Litt le Ed" and "as a child",

The Measure of the Truth I seek.

But now I must decrease, that He,

Yeshua, may "increase" to be the "More",

The "All-in-all", of all my highest, true Desire.

The nations, in the balance, hang

On every Word that God performs.

77.

Seventy-seven says it all:

"Double your pleasure, double your fun"

And RUMInate on what God sends.

Be ever coming into More

And, 'Chew on this', to "taste and see"

How Good Love Is,
"Seated" above....
I hang on every Word He says

As Double-Portions of I AM.

78.

Seventy-eight:

A New Beginning every day,

To enter into Perfect Rest.

The Promises of God
Are True,

"Yes and Amen"

In all ways

And, for all Time,

Real.

I pray we all have eyes to see

And ears to hear

And hearts to speak

Of seeking Him

And fi nding More

Than we have known

To be, "of God",

The Substance

Of our deep Desire.

79.

"We wrestle not with flesh and blood."

Our warfare is not with our own

But with the lies

That Mankind

On the whole

Has bought.

Just ask the birds and animals.

Just ask the sea.

Just ask the sky.

Look to the heavens that declare

The Glory of the One True God.

Their Wisdom goes forth day and night.

The Love that they declare is free

And yet it costs us Life to live.

I have but one, to give to You.

You are the Lover of my soul

And I am Yours And You are Mine.

It is MORE than enough Of this.

And so I enter into More.

"Let there be More" Echoes in me.

80.

I will Return

To You Who are

The Word of God

Sent unto Man.

I hear You whisper in my ear:

"Receive and then, Go, freely Give.

Such as I have, I give to you

To give away

As freely as the lilies grow.

Have I not clothed you with My Light?

Have I not bathed you in My Word?

Have I not called you to be Mine?

Do not My Waters turn to Wine?

Come, drink your fill

To thirst no more.

Be ever being filled

With MORE.

Why wait

While it is still today?"

81.

"Let 'all God's children' come to Me.

Go gather them; go feed My sheep.

Permit them all to come and eat

To drink their fill

From Waters still

To be at Peace

Under the Shadow of

My wing,

Under My arm

To find that I AM full of Love.

Permit them all

To come "as children", as they are,

The sheep of pastures that are Mine.

The Earth is Mine

And all the Fullness found thereof

To be the Nesting Place of Love.

Call them to come; give voice and whistle

In My Name

To "be come in", just as they are

Both young and old,

In every 'state' that's known to man,

From every nation, tongue and tribe

To all be one, to be "as one", as I AM One

With many facets, each to shine.

off er something wholly new.

Eternal Life is Mine to off er as

I AM. Receiving you, they will get Me.

The More they want, the More they get.

Throughout the ages, I repeat, always the same:

The Life that's in My Blood, "in you"

Is freely given you to share.

The More you share, the More it grows

To be the Magnum Dream of God That you can live out

In My Name.

Again I say, the Life that's in

My Blood "in you"

Remains the same throughout all Time -

The DNA entwining you, unseen, with MORE

Of My "True Vine",

the Mystery of the Christ, in you

Plants you to be as "Israel"

The vineyard on a hill, that's Mine."

*****

"Hineni, LORD", remains my cry; send us to Yours.

Or, bett er yet, send them to us;

Permit them, Lord, to come to Yours

Into our arms, as Israel, returning home.

I bear the Witness of such Wealth

That carries souls across vast seas

Returning home, to Israel.

We am commissioned, thus to sail,

To 'set sail' and to 'spread our wings'

To carry them, to bear them closer to I AM,

Through You, through Seas of Loss, to Joy.

To Joy that ever is our Strength.

To Feast with You, to see You and to take

You in To Tabernacle, with us, here,

Enveloped in the Fire of Love.

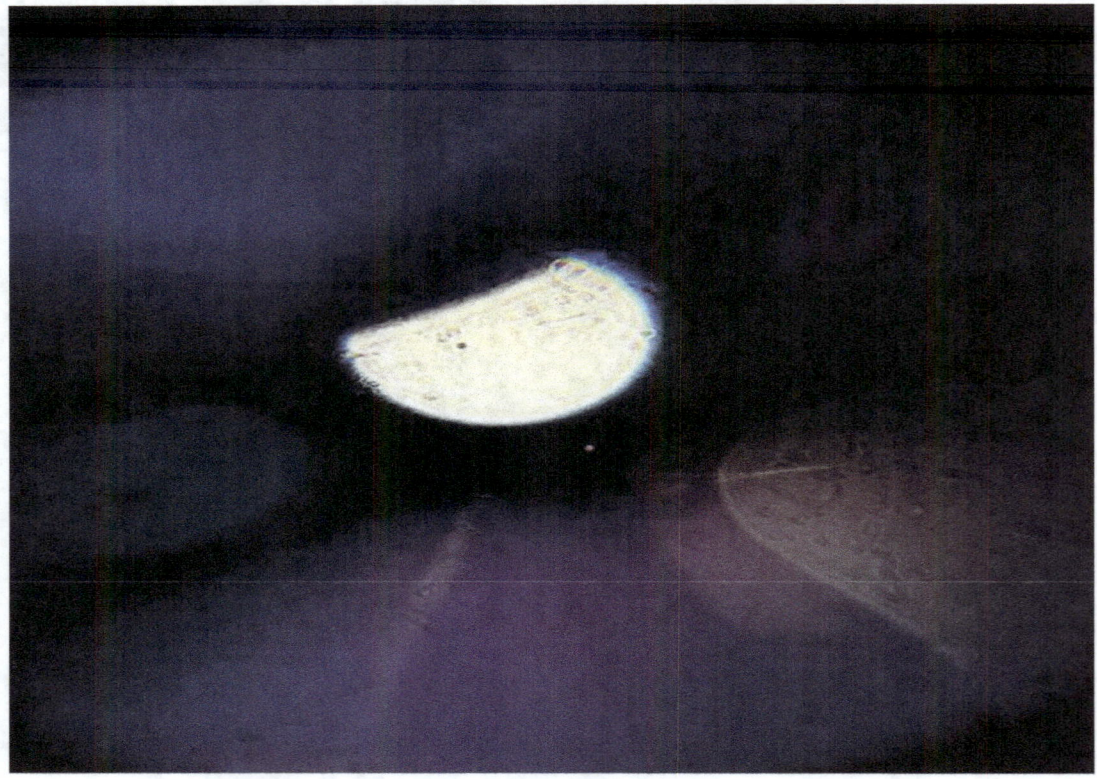

82.

Come, dance with me.

Ignite us with the Love of God, With "tongues of fire"

With Life upon our tongues to speak

Of More of You than we have known.

Make all as jealous as we are

For More of You than we have known

That we, together, may come up

And worship, without fear,

the LORD.

Deliver us from fear of death And fear of man

And give us, Lord, the Sword of Your Word,

Sharp and quick

To cut away

The fett ers than have held us back.

Come circumcise our hearts for this -

To Enter In, within the Door, within Your side

Behind the veil which hides Your Face,

Within Your Heart

To be made New

And, "Come forth"

as Your "wife of youth",

the "Second Adam" by our sides.

To come forth leaning on Your arm.

Let it be so!

Let there be More!

I know that You have heard my cries.

83.

Your arm around us is a wall,

A Harbor arm, the Shelter of the Rock in storm.

Within Your lea, we ride storm out.

The seas may roar, but on your tongue

Is, "Peace! Be still!

Be gathered here, beneath My wing.

There's More to come:

The very best and worst of days.

Take Refuge where you are

And live.

Do not depart from Me again.

Do not shrink back to be destroyed.

But, rest here, in My arms, for Good.

It's bett er that you fall in Love

Than be, in hate, consumed by loss.

Let there be More; the choice is yours.

I Am your Shield and Great Reward

For things 'impossible', well done.

What can you not do in My Name

To hear Me say, "Well done" to you.

"More than a servant, come My friend;

Seeking for lovers, I found you.

Now you are Mine and I am yours.

With Me all things are possible.

And those who know Me, shall be called

To go, do exploits in My Name.

My Joy shall be your Strength in More

That yet remains to be revealed.

84.

Vengeance is Mine; I will repay.

Continue in My Kindness, rest.

Rest in My Kindness; be at Peace.

My, "Peace! Be still!" will be enough.

I give you My Peace, as a rose.

Its petals strew the path you walk.

The blossoms of it crown your past.

But more buds yet will open up

Into the Fullness of My Love.

Continue on

To be "no more"

As Enoch was.

I carry you

Where you could never go alone.

And I-AM-With-you

Through it all.

Always the same, I always reassure

With More."

85.

Your "arm" around us is a Wall,

Salvation's "walls", the "arm" of God

Both seen and unseen, here, with us

And we, within Your arms, are more

Than we could ever be, alone.

Here, we, within You, form the same -

A Western, Wailing Wall of prayer,

A wall of "living stones" that stand

Against the darkness now that spreads

The lies the world believes as truth.

You are the Truth.

In You, we stand and, war against

The wickedness "in high places"

That overshadow us with threats.

Death threats abound.

But Your Love, greater, Wins the Day.

Hidden in You, beneath the Shadow of Your wing

We "come forth"

"More than conquerors"

And Death is swallowed up by LIFE.

You are that Life that opens up our graves

And calls,

Knows us by name.

We are "engraved" upon Your palms.

Your hands read like an open Book.

Our names are "writt en" in

Your Blood And Life is in the Blood You shed.

86.

You are to us the Tree of Life

And with Your Sap, we have been sealed.

We have been sealed both in and out:

We wear You on our arm, a Seal.

You are the Star, from Jacob came To be the Banner over us.

And here You are within our hearts,

Abiding as the Word of God,

The Inner and the Outer, One.

Lift up a stone and there You are.

And turn a page and You are here.

Open our hearts and find Your Seed.

Men now get Pregnant with the Son

And are "with child"

And groan with Labor Pains of More.

The Birth Pangs of Messiah grow.

What shall we bring forth? Heaven knows.

Can these bones live? Thou knowest LORD

And You are One.

You build us up to be Your house.

We are a Wailing Wall of stones.

Within our cracks, we place our prayers,

Our very lives,

Our hearts of longing after You

To be here, with us, 'after all'.

You hear our cries

And have come down,

A "man of sorrows" just like ours.

87.

Come, find Your place of rest, in us.

Come, make Your bed within our hearts

That we may Know the

Love of God And rise up, pregnant with

Your Word. For "unto us a child is born", A "son is given"

In YOUR Name.

In Him we find YOUR Gift of Life.

It is Enough and More by far

To know that YOU are One with Him.

It is Enough and More than this,

Than what is writt en in this book;

The Joy remains "unspeakable".

The Mystery is of "Christ in you",

The Living Word, alive, in us.

Come, and be More than we have Known.

Reveal Yourself as having been revealed to us.

Come lay Your head upon our breasts

For You have cradled us as Yours.

We have not Known Love as Love Is,

That feeds, from birth to death, the soul

With sweet Communion with I AM

The Bread from Heaven coming down

And Wine of the Beloved, poured.

Here on the course set by the Wind,

We are propelled by Yours, the Breath,

To cross the Threshold in Your arms.

Thus far, have You not carried us?

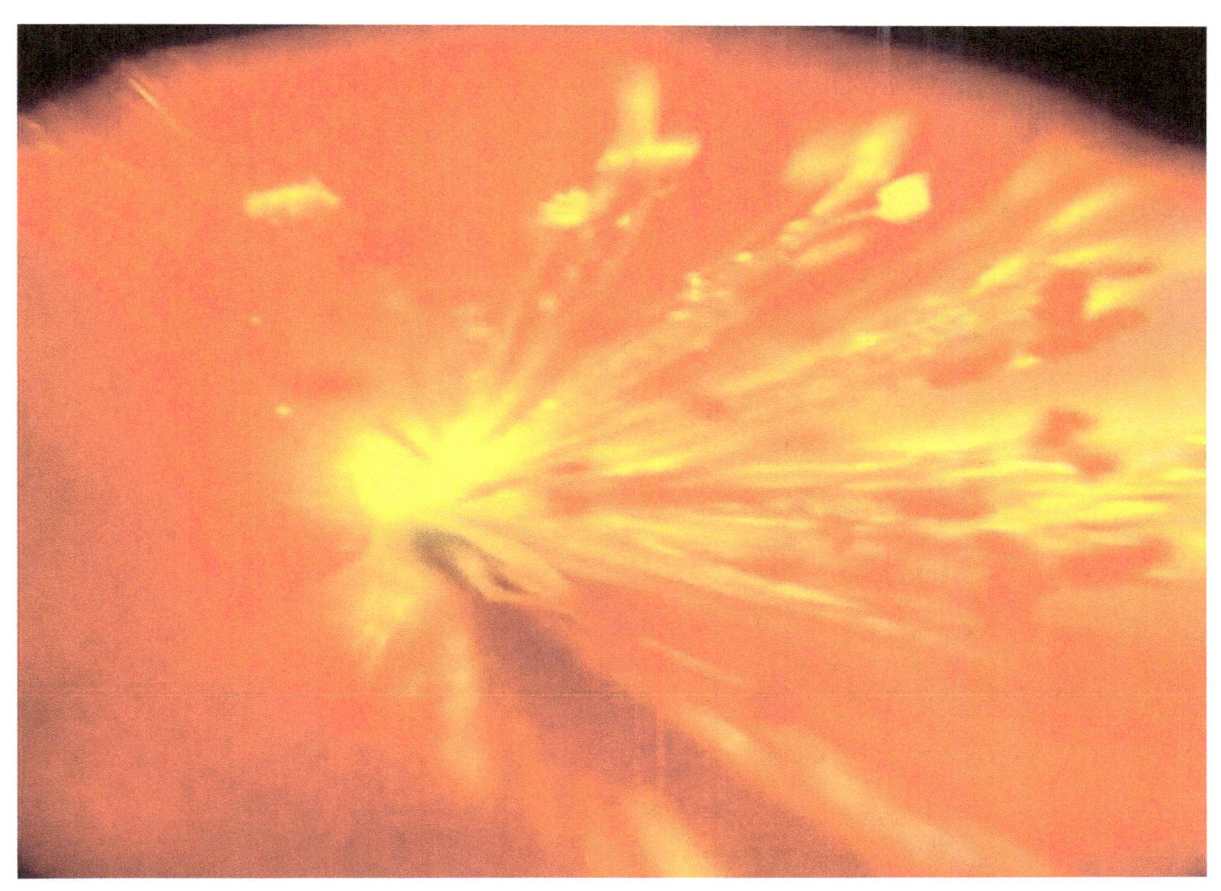

88.

Carried "In the Direction of the Wind",

These are Your "Footprints in the Sand"

And You have been the Open Door.

We have not come this far alone.

"You, sitt ing in My Garden, here

With ears to hear of Love revealed

And hearts to know

The Voice that comes this way to you,

Now let Me also hear your voice.

Do not keep silent any more:

For such a time as this you come...

Into 'your own' Inheritance, unto 'your own',

To be your brother's keeper, Mine,

To shepherd flocks for slaughter, "marked"

By nations that ignore My Plans

In favor of the plans they make.

Do not go with them where they go.

Come, follow Me, to be a fisher after souls."

*****

Come, show Yourself; oh, my Beloved, be revealed.

Be manifest just as You are: "Just as I am", I come undone.

Come on the clouds, and

Rain on us, until we overflow with

You, until we flow, "as one", with

More, with More of You and less of us.

'Till "streams" from in us rise and shine

To be "the light" that You call forth as "born again"

Throughout the Earth, to make Jerusalem "a praise".

May we ascend, singing of You

The Song of Songs

Within thy gates, Jerusalem.

May we be found there, worshipping.

With You, within our midst, revealed.

Come quickly, Lord.

"Quickly, I come."

Amen. So be it. May it be

That... "next year in Jerusalem..."

Is here.

And may Your people be a bride,

A "wife of youth",

Rejoicing in the streets with JOY.

Pour out Your Miracle of Love, of Oil,

Of More to come.

I live and move and have my being

Here

In seeking

More of You.

A stranger in my own far land.

Appearing
 FEAR is this way:
"False
Evidence
Appearing
Real"
To us
FAITH is as Substance always was, our
"Father
Always
Is
True
Hope".

Some things, appearing "Finished", aren't.

The Way goes ever from the Door, Across

each Threshold, into More:

Such Love is casting, "all fear", out.

"More Love" awaits the heart that seeks,

The hand that knocks upon The Door, The

tongue, that "speaking Life", asks You.

With "More to come", I ask You, "Enter in

To these."

I give You my "best"; give us Yours.

I know You have and always will.

I thank You, Father, for Your Word.

"With great mercies will I gather thee."

Isaiah 54

MASTER, HOW CLOSE?

With mercies will I gather thee

through valleys and o'er mountain tops

through wilderness and across seas

to bring you to a place prepared

where you shall then "BE STILL AND KNOW",

where you shall kneel, and trembling, rise

where I shall visit you in song.

Fear not, my own: my perfect love casts Fear aside

I come to breathe on all my own.

You shall inhale the Promise, come.

You shall be filled to overfl ow.

We shall be close, and be as one

For I have called and you have come.

"Break forth into singing...
for Thy Maker is thine
husband" and "this is as
the waters of Noah."
Isaiah 54

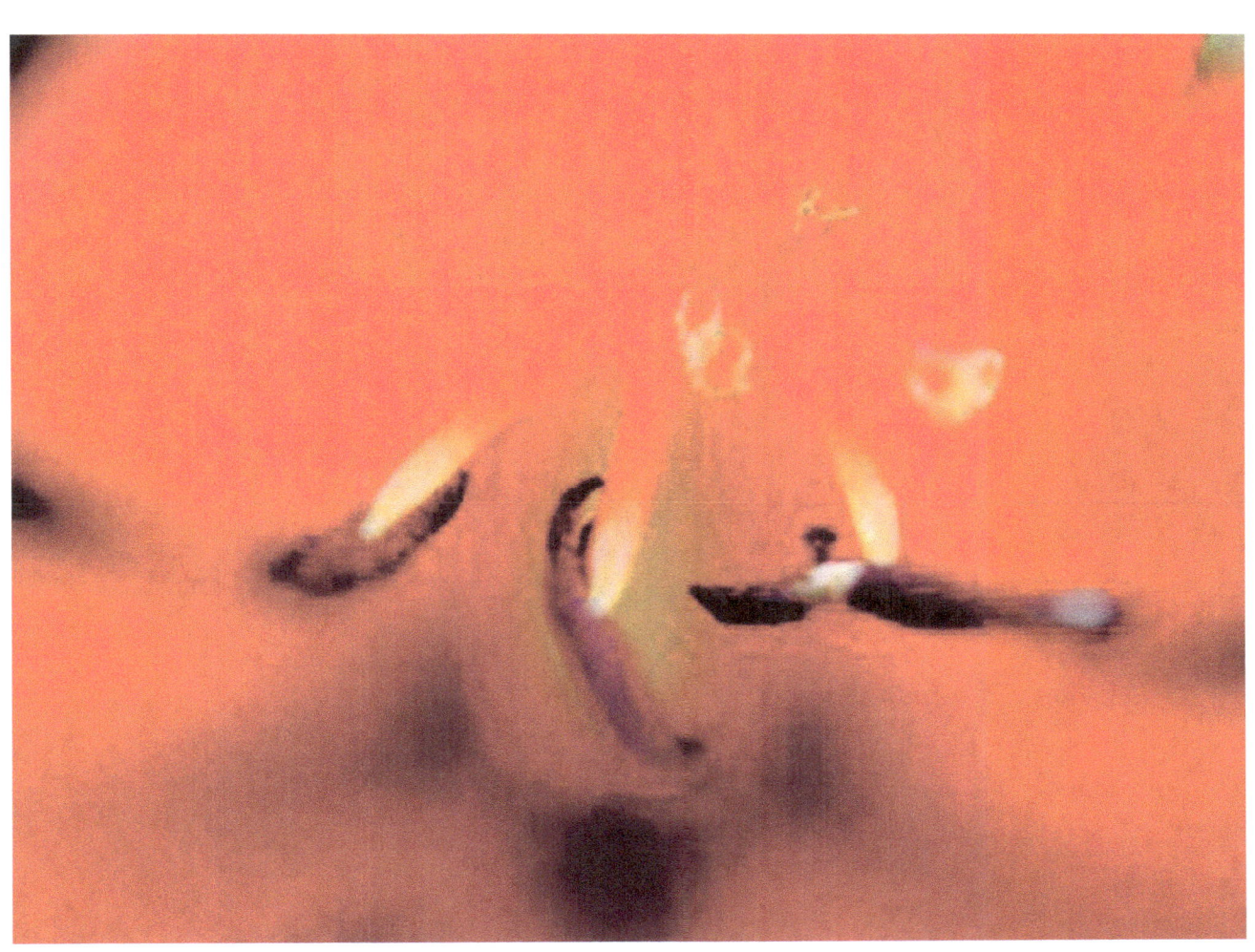

Society of Noah

"For the earth shall be filled with the knowledge of the glory of the Lord, as the waters cover the sea."
Habakkuk 2:14

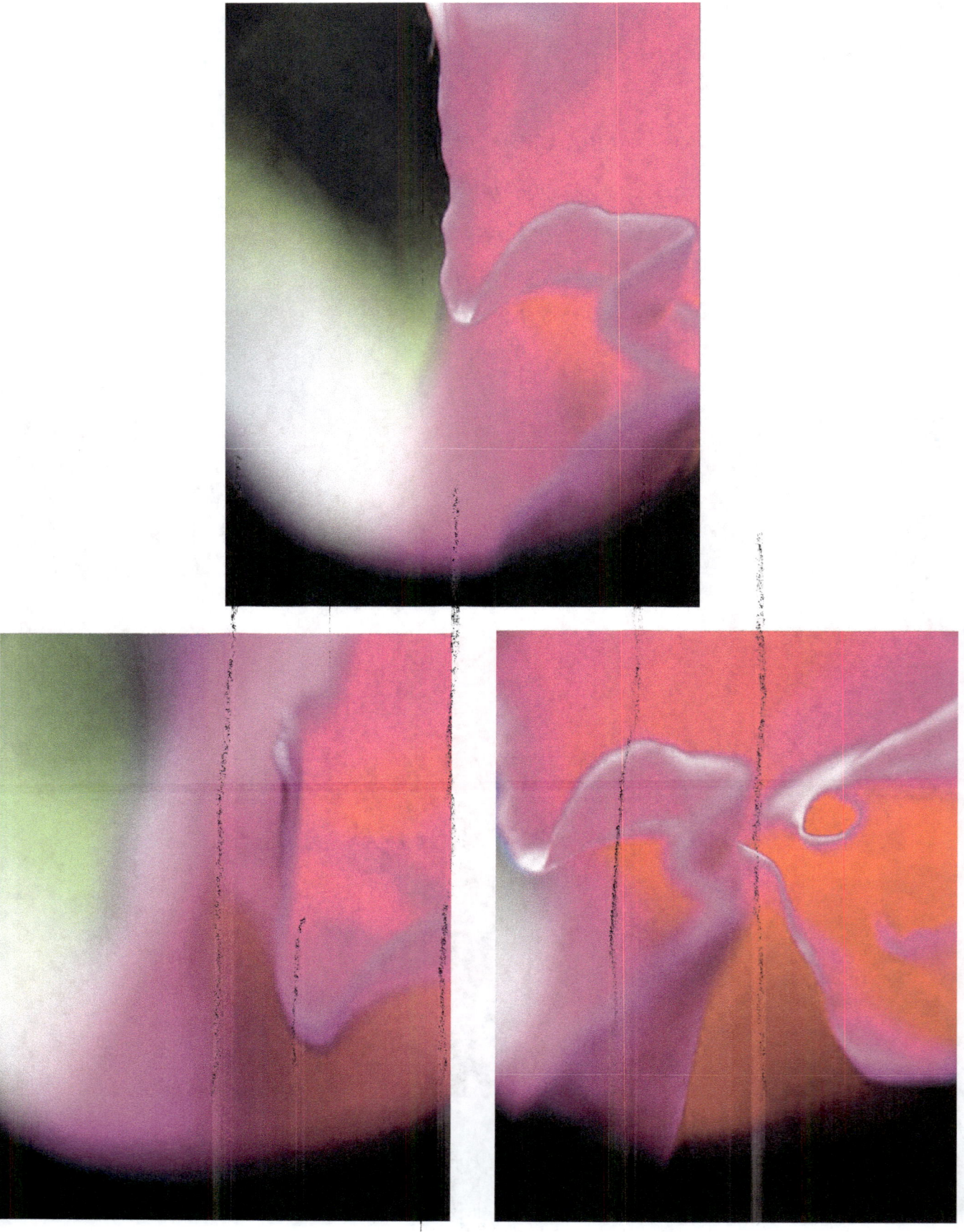

"...with a rainbow above.... and on His head are many crowns." -Revelation 10:1; 19:12.

"I open up a Mystery: When I return, I will not wear a crown of thorns. I will be crowned with many crowns, formed of the blossoms of My Love, My Loving-Kindness given you; wherewith in life, I have crowned you with many crowns. Behold, I come, unto My own where My face has been formed in you to scent the world with Love-made-known, with Who I Am, the Mystery of the Word made flesh, revealed to be "in you" with Words, with "Christ in you". As it is written, so it is. Amen. Thus says the Lord, rejoicing over you in song, in love."

"And I saw a new heaven and a new earth: for the first heaven and the first earth were passed away.... And I John saw the holy city, new Jerusalem, coming down from God out of heaven, prepared as a bride adorned for her husband. And I heard a great voice out of heaven saying, Behold, the tabernacle of God is with mne, and he will dwell with them, and they shall be his people, and God himself shall be with them, and be their God. And God shall wipe away all tears from their eyes; and there shall be no more death, neither sorrow , nor crying, neither shall there be any more pain for the former things are passed away. And he that sat upon the throne said, Behold, I make all things new. And he said unto me, Write: for these words are true and faithful. And he said unto me, It is done. I am Alpha and Omege, the beginning and the end. I will give unto him that is athirst of the fountain of the water of life freely. He that overcometh shall inherit all things; and I will be his God, and he shall be my son." - KJV, Revelation 21:1-7